A Sense of Place

A Sense of Place

Margaret A. Westlie

Selkirk
STORIES

TABLE OF CONTENTS

A Sense of Place

A Sense of Place

I feel as if I have been away at least a decade as I peer out the window of the plane. In fact, it has been only five days. We are flying in low and circling over Prince Edward Island for our landing at Charlottetown, the island's capital. From this height, I can see the whole of Prince Edward Island nestled in the curve of Nova Scotia and New Brunswick. It is surrounded, this cold March day, by the grey ice that covers the Northumberland Strait every winter. Black angular tracks have been opened by the icebreakers on their daily trips carrying passengers and goods to and from the mainland. Tiny specks move about on the surface of the ice. The seals are still wintering here. Directly below me I can see the fields still covered in snow, but beginning to melt around the edges. The fifteen feet of snow we received this winter is beginning to soften and disappear. It should be gone by May. The fences around the fields give them the appearance of having been sewn together. The red clay roads that have been plowed free of snow are a bright border to this tidy quilt. The black asphalt of the Trans Canada highway winds its way from the ferries into Charlottetown. I think back to younger, warmer times.

I waken slowly and lie for some minutes in the warm nest of bed under the eaves. Downstairs I can hear the gentle rumble of my grandfather's voice and the softer tones of my grandmother as she answers. The stove lid rattles as someone adds another stick to the fire, and presently the screen door in the porch slams with the distinctive rat-a-tat from the metal loop that is its outside handle.

My eyes play games with the wallpaper. I follow the pattern spaces around trying to get from the part where it disappears behind the bed, upwards past the wrinkle that isn't supposed to be there, without crossing any lines. From the front yard comes the faint screech of the pump handle, faster at first, then slowing as the pump begins to pull water from the deep well. The screech becomes a clunk as the load becomes heavier until the sound is lost in the gush of water into the pail.

My eyes make it to the top of the wallpaper and I follow the border around to where it passes the jigsaw puzzle picture assembled and framed when my uncles were boys. I study again the bright flag of my aunt's almost victory in a fiddling contest in Ontario. "I was up against the likes of King Gannon," I remember her complaining once. "He knows all the fancy moves to catch the judges' eyes. I know I can play better than he does. You had to be from Ontario to win anyway." I can tell that the loss is still sour in her mouth.

A soft breeze through the window moves the curtains. It brings with it the sweet scent of drying hay overlaid with the richer smell of manure. The whole is carried on the clear salt tang of ocean air. In the row of birches in the front yard the birds chirp and call. A long piercing whistle followed by four question marks of sound is answered from the spruce bush across the field. I think about the birches. My mother's voice tells the story. "Daddy dug them up in the woods one day, the summer after we moved here. We hauled water for them all that summer. Buckets and buckets. We thought at first they weren't going to live, but they did, all five of them."

I hear my Uncle John stirring in the room by the top of the stairs. He is home from Ontario for his vacation, as are Aunt Florence, and Aunt Eleanor and her husband Emery. Uncle John and my sister will likely go fishing today. I quell the sudden surge of jealousy with the thought that I don't like to fish anyway, but the tightness of envy remains in my throat.

My sister has already gone downstairs. I picture her hurrying past the darkness of the green blind which provides my grandparents with a closet under the eaves just outside our door. Ghosts and hobgoblins can hide in that darkness. I always hurry past it too. Years later my sister would waken in the darkest hours to see a shadowy white figure standing by the foot of the bed. She would shut her eyes tightly against the sight, then wonder in the morning if she had been dreaming.

I hear my grandfather talking to my grandmother in the pantry. He's planning a trip to the mill this morning. I leap out of bed and dress hurriedly. He'll take us with him if we ask. Maybe he'll let us drive the horse! I race downstairs past the green blind, no thoughts of ghosts in my mind now.

That evening all the relatives assemble for the music. Uncle John, Aunt Florence, Aunt Eleanor, Uncle Mac and Uncle Emery are all there. Some neighbours join us too. My grandfather, to tease me, tells them about the adventure to the mill and how I almost drove Tidy into the ditch. I duck my head in embarrassment.

Everyone gathers in the parlour because that's where the organ is. Uncle John plays the organ by ear. He plays for dances down in Montague when he's home. My grandmother is fond of saying that he only ever had a quarter of lessons and he can play anything. Aunt Florence plays her fiddle, and Uncle Mac plays the guitar. He made a mandolin once and they all say that it played very well.

Music and talk fill the parlour and spill out into the rest of the house. "Play 'Red Wing,'" someone says. "Play 'Rubber Dolly,'" calls someone else. "How about 'Golden Wedding Reel?'"

Uncle Mac strums a few chords on the guitar and Aunt Florence tries the tune of the fiddle with the organ and presently the melodies roll forth again. It's hard to keep my feet still. If only I could play like that, I think. I want to dance but the small fussy room filled with neighbours and relatives and stuffed furniture is too small. Uncle Mac and Aunt Florence sing a duet. It seems like magic that they can blend their voices and their instruments and sing the words all at the same time. The songs tell a story. Aunt Florence takes the guitar from Uncle Mac and sings a song she made up one day. Her song tells about how two brothers went hunting and one got shot. Everyone applauds. It's a sad song and I spend some time thinking about it.

"I guess it's time to put the kettle on," my grandmother says and gets up from her chair. My Aunt Eleanor goes to help her. "Big John MacNeil," "Swamp Lake Breakdown," and "Johnny Waggoner," with all its double stops, dance out from Aunt Florence's fiddle. She really could have won that contest if she'd been from Ontario, I think. Another tune and then my grandmother's voice calls us to the kitchen for a bite to eat.

"Sit in everyone and help yourselves, there's lots more where that came from," says my grandmother. She begins pouring tea. They've pulled the kitchen table, with its red and white oilcloth cover, away from the wall and raised both leaves to accommodate all the people. Plates of crusty homemade bread covered in new butter go from hand to hand. Apple jelly from their own orchard shimmers redly in the pressed glass bowl. "I boil the red apple skins for colour," my grandmother says. She's proud of her jelly.

I coat my bread with molasses until it drips off the edge. "D'you think you have enough?" Uncle John teases. "Here, have a little more." He goes to pour more molasses onto my bread. I squeal and turn away and stuff the remainder hastily into my mouth, then smirk at him through sticky lips. Grandma passes the cookies around. They're her own sugar cookies with a raisin on top. I eat all around the raisin to save it for the last bite. It always tastes a little burnt and funny, but I like it anyway. She offers more tea.

"It's time you 'childern' were in bed," my grandmother says. Her mispronunciation of children is always a curiosity to me. I think about it as I climb the stairs and hurry past the secrets of the dark green blind and reach for the string to turn on the light. I hurry into my nightgown and climb into bed pulling the light string as I go. Downstairs the music begins again and I can hear them laughing at some incomprehensible foolishness from Aunt Florence. I lie in the dark trying to hear what they're saying, but it's too far away, and soon I am asleep.

The plane bumps gently onto the runway. Times are different now, and life has changed. Aunt Florence's fiddle is silent and music no longer flows from the parlour in Kilmuir as it once did. She died young and lies with her parents and grandparents in the Valleyfield cemetery. In my mind's ear I can hear her laugh and play "Big John MacNeil" once again.

Living on an Island

I live on Prince Edward Island, that little bow tie on the east coast of Canada. It would take a long day's drive to get from North Cape to East Point with much varied landscape in between. It is very fertile land and will grow almost anything that can survive the climate. Winters can be very harsh with snow up past the eaves. My young cousins were coasting down the slope of the roof into the yard last winter. It will make wonderful memories for them in these days of global warming.

Prince Edward Island has changed a great deal since I was a child. New faces, new ways and lots of company from foreign lands. It's educational and sometimes a little unsettling, but we extend a welcome to everyone. At least, most of us do. It is still a lovely place to live and much more interesting for the diversity. So welcome all, whether you come for a lifetime or just a visit.

An interesting point about living on an island is that you can't get lost. It has sides. You can only go so far before you run into ocean and you have to turn around or get your feet wet. While I was living inland for so many years I longed for the circumference of place that the Island provided.

I felt as if I were a broken egg with no shell to define my edges and that I was liable to run if I didn't keep tight hold of my container. I missed the neighbourliness of people here, even when I didn't know them. I was away for thirty years but found that it still existed after all this time. To my mind this signifies Island living.

Sleeping Outdoors

When we were children we never missed an opportunity to sleep outdoors. It seemed so free and fresh. There was almost a wildness to it that didn't exist indoors. A throwback to our caveman ancestors perhaps?

There was a luminosity to it. The night sky was never completely dark, the moon and the great wash of stars in the Milky Way saw to that. The sky behind them was like dark blue velvet and seemed never-ending. It gave me a feeling of butterflies in my stomach with its vastness. I wondered where it went and what was at the end of it. I tried to imagine it once, but the prospect was almost frightening in its enormity. I could never reach the edge. One thing I realized was that from any point in the enormity of space I could always be found if they knew my address. This was a wonderful realization because I could never get lost.

There was never a sense of danger sleeping out of doors. Of course, we didn't do this in the city, but here on the Island my cousins lived on a farm far from roads and other farms. The threat from strangers was less then too, and we, as children, never had to consider any of that, nor the adults who allowed us to do it.

Sometimes we would string a blanket up with clothespins, sometimes we'd just sleep under the stars. We'd throw an old quilt on the ground to cushion ourselves from the packed red clay, occasional round pebble and tufts of grass, and all was well in our small worlds. The dog would join us when he wasn't hunting.

I remember once, quite late at night, but before the adults went to bed, a thunderstorm blew up. At first it was just a gentle rumble, still distant, but coming nearer. We lay and watched the flickering lights until the raindrops started. After the first few drops we decided that indoors was best, at least for that night.

At Grandma's House

At my grandmother's house in Kinross, Prince Edward Island, my sister and I occupied a bedroom on the back. It had a window on the side that gave a good view of the Murray Harbour Road. We slept in a very old bed with a heavy headboard carved in various fruits surrounded by ribbons, a veritable cornucopia all in wood. Our windows were open to the fresh air and in the morning I could lie there listening to the many birds that lived in the trees by the lane singing for the joy of another summer day.

Sam Stoney's store was situated on the corner of the Murray Harbour Road and the Kinross Road. Sometimes a car went down to the store or farther, running over the red gravel road already worn to washboard despite having been graded only a few weeks before. It scattered pebbles as large as marbles, larger even, and sent them pinging and dinging onto the side or into the ditch. Cars trailed a cloud of pink dust as fine as powdered sugar behind themselves. I wondered where they were really going.

I thought of the shadowy interior of Sam's store. The sound of the screen door with its thin spring slamming it behind a customer as it banged and bounced open again then came to rest in its frame to await the next customer coming or going. The scarred counter with its equally scarred bench along the front had a hinged top that held unknown treasures.

May, Sam's wife, tended the counter and sorted the daily mail and newspapers and was willing to break open a packet of Wrigley's gum and sell it for a penny a stick—only the original flavours, of course. She also sold us children half popsicles for five cents, breaking them apart with her strong hands. May also taught piano. My purchases were always either the stick of gum or the half popsicle—orange, lime ricky or sometimes grape. I think there was also a limited supply of candy, but I wasn't interested in that.

The store smelled of tobacco, usually Hickey and Nicholson's twist, redolent of molasses, but plug tobacco as well. Leather harness adorned the rafters in case anyone had need of it. It smelled of whale oil and dust. In the back room was a supply of feed for farm animals adding its own dusty odour to the mix. Kerosene could be had for the oil lamps that were still in use across the Island. Its oily, gassy scent overlay it all.

Sam's store is long gone now by about fifty or sixty years. May and Sam too. Sam died at my uncle's fighting a house fire that ultimately burned the house to the ground. The chimney exploded from the heat and he took one of the bricks to his head and died almost instantly. It was a great loss to the community. May lived on and eventually died of old age.

CHOCOLATE FUDGE

In some places it is a custom to exchange plates of cookies and other treats with the neighbours at Christmas time. I have been rather sporadic about it, so it is always a lovely surprise when someone arrives at my door with such a delightful treat.

This year I decided to make fudge. It had been calling to me for several months and I debated it, how much, to whom, when, do I have time? You know the drill. Once I decided that I was going to do it, I had to find a recipe, which I did, and the fudge turned out well. I cut it up and shared it among several plates, covered them with plastic wrap, and in the evening we began paying short calls on our neighbours.

One neighbour got rather a surprise. Their house looks like the one next door in the dark. We didn't know these people but when you are already on the doorstep with the bell rung and the door opening from the inside, it's too late to do anything but smile and say: "Hello, we're your neighbours," and hand them the plate of fudge with a "Merry Christmas." Never mind, I'm glad we did. It was a very pleasant visit and we met some nice people whom we didn't even know lived nearby. It was a lovely Christmas present to us.

Of course, this is not the first time we've done such a thing. Once we were invited to share Christmas dinner with a friend and I agreed to bring dessert. I had only been to her house once. It was in a subdivision where all the houses looked alike except for some very minor differences. I was sure we were at the right house and walked right in, dessert in hand and set it on the counter. We called out in a friendly manner and strangers came rushing up from the downstairs family room, alarm written all over their faces. We apologized as graciously as we knew how and explained the circumstances, then grabbed dessert, wished them Merry Christmas, got directions and fled.

COMMUNITY

Uncle Harold was in a story telling mood, and I get a lot of my story ideas from him. I think he may be the oldest living relative I have now. His mother lived to be 106, so I hope he takes after her. I very much enjoy my visits with him. He knows old gossip from the nineteenth century and he knows who is related and how.

Community is so important. It gives us value and a sense of place. I remember once I went to a ceilidh (an informal Scottish social gathering) and the woman I was sitting next to began quizzing me suspiciously on my pedigree. It's an Island thing. Once I told her that I was the granddaughter of Margaret MacLeod, who was well known in the community, everything was fine. I was okay. Mind you, I have no idea who the woman was and only saw her on that one occasion.

I heard a similar story the other day. The woman had lived on the Island for 45 years and had had one of her children here. An old man was doing the genealogy thing and asked her where she was from. When she said Nova Scotia, she was immediately suspect as an off-islander, a foreigner, if you will. She told about her son being born here, and he considered the situation in silence for a few minutes, then said: "Ah, yes, but was he conceived here?"

Our genealogy is a sad thing to lose but I fear that it is slipping away from us in this age of computers and jobs elsewhere both in Canada and abroad. We need to hold onto it so that we don't lose our sense of having a place.

Learning to Milk

I learned to milk when I was six years old. I begged and begged my grandfather to show me how. The ritual begins with going to the pasture to bring in the cows. The procedure began about seven o'clock, just as the sun was setting in glorious pinks and yellows. The air was sweet with the smell of ripening hay. The hard-packed road with patches of red sand was cool on my bare feet. At the pasture gate my grandfather would call: "Cup! Cup!" I still don't know why the "cup." In a minute or so the cows would come from away down the field near the woods where they had wandered during the warmth of the day. They lumbered slowly across the field, tails switching against the flies and black flies, their udders heavy with abundant rich milk. They knew where home was and led the way. I kept a safe distance because my grandfather's cows had horns, and he had already scared me to safe distances with stories of what those horns could do.

At last my begging to learn to milk paid off. My grandfather sat me down on a three legged stool with a small saucepan from Grandma's pantry in one hand and a teat in the other. As I was instructed in the art of milking the cow swung her great head around to see what was going on. She knew that I was a novice and held very still.

What a thrill when the first tiny stream of milk appeared in the bottom of the saucepan. I milked a few ounces that night. My hands were only six years old and had no strength but I was so proud—I'd learned to milk. Eventually I graduated to a bucket held between my skinny knees. With my head tucked into the curve of the cow's warm flank and the cats swarming around my ankles I could milk a few inches into the bucket. Peace and tranquility suffused my being as I learned the joy of milking.

MAKING CREAM

The separator was a great ungainly beast that stood in the shadowy coolness of the back porch. It was always covered with a clean tea towel and it seemed mysterious and a little scary to my childish imagination. After the milking was done, Grandma would pour the milk from the milk bucket into the big metal bowl with a spigot at the bottom, on top of the beast. She would then bring the beast to life by turning the long crank on the side and it would begin to hum more loudly and its pitch would become higher and higher. The accompanying bell would ding regularly, keeping the beat for the process. As the turning crank added more and more power to the procedure the bell would grow fainter and fainter until it finally disappeared.

The beast seemed almost to take on a life of its own, and it became easier to turn the crank. When the dinging bell faded to silence my grandmother would open the spigot on the side of the bowl and the milk would flow in a narrow stream over a series of discs enclosed in the machine. Then, almost magically to me, the milk flowed out of one long spout into a container and the cream flowed out of another. I have no idea how the magic happened, all I know is that the big can was filled with milk and the little can was filled with cream. These cans were kept cool until it was time to set them on the side of the road very early in the morning where they were soon picked up by a truck and taken, clanking together with all the other cans of milk and cream, to the dairy in Montague.

Where it went after that I had no notion. I don't think I ever heard. I just remember that when I was at home in the city, the milk wagon would come by every morning. The horse pulled the yellow Farmers' Dairy wagon to the top of the hill leaving a "present" for us at the top every day. The milkman would come into the kitchen with a carrier filled with clinking glass milk and cream bottles for my mother's perusal. Milk was only a few cents a quart then, and the bottles were closed with cardboard caps with tiny tabs that the boys would collect to play caps with once they were dried. I played caps once, against the side of the house with my friend Nicky. I wasn't very good so I don't think I won. I was only a girl after all.

Making Music

Not long ago we participated in a Variety Concert at church. It was a benefit to refurbish the beautiful pipe organ in the sanctuary which was thirty-five years old and being held together with duct tape and prayer. Lately there had been some interesting sounds coming out of it but Susan, our organist, was becoming quite adept at avoiding those keys. However, we could see the day coming when she would have too few keys left on which to play a complete hymn. The picture I have in my mind just now is "interesting."

We have some very talented people in our choir, both singers and instrumentalists. A community chorus also uses the sanctuary to rehearse and give performances in and took part in the evening as well. Also trios, quartets and solo performers. We even had a witch do a number, as well as a soft shoe act. Both sacred and secular music was presented and the choir gave a rockin' rendition of "Leaning on the Everlasting Arms," which we repeated the next morning in church for those who couldn't attend. Those who had already heard it just had to endure. I think they survived as we got an very nice ovation.

Music is such fun to create even if all you do is play the comb. It can be created anywhere, any time and all it takes is a few people who can put it together. *Ceilidhs* and Kitchen Parties are spontaneous and draw people together. Stories and jokes are told, news is exchanged, who's getting married, who's had the latest grand baby, who is sick unto death and do the families need anything. The life of the community is nourished and supported by musical events. And the amazing thing is it always seems to come out of thin air. It's magic!

SHARING THE NEWS

Colouring. Who'd have thought? I was at a colouring party the other afternoon. It seems frivolous but it is a lovely, peaceful pastime. There were five of us and we sat and chatted, drank tea, coloured and shared the news.

You have to understand that news is not gossip. Gossip implies a certain maliciousness of spirit, a mean glee at another's misfortunes. News is the glue that holds community together. The kind of uplifting that conveys a sense of place and sharing of burdens. It is active participation in another's woes. The kind of participation that brings out casseroles and cookies for the afflicted. We acknowledge their distress through news and then pull together to remedy the situation as best we can. It may not be perfect but at least it surrounds the unhappy one with comfort and a padded framework to lean on until he can gather his strength for the next pull on the oars.

Haying

It is summer. The sun burns down from a clear, blue sky. Locusts whine in the spruce trees by the barn. I try to run barefoot across the hayfield but the stubble is sharp on my city feet. I slow and try sliding my feet below the tops of the cut grass. It helps, but only a little. I'm too small to be of much use in the hay field but I go anyway because I'm young and curious about everything.

I watch Peter, the black horse, pull the truck wagon across the field. He seems to know when to move and how far to go with just a shout from my grandfather. Uncle John, home from Ontario for his holidays, stands on top of the wagon receiving the forkfuls of hay and building the load. He is directed occasionally by shouts from the others: "A little more here, a little less there. No! No! It's getting lopsided." It's the first time I've ever heard the word "lopsided," and I store it for future thought.

Finally the load is built to everyone's satisfaction and we head back to the barn. Someone hoists me up on top for the ride. I sit in the middle of the load amid the itchy, fragrant hay. Uncle John sits down behind me to ensure that I don't fall off. The load moves over the ruts in the lane, the rolling sensation not unlike riding on the back of a big horse. Much shouting as the load catches on the gatepost into the barnyard, and we leave a tuft of hay like uncombed hair on top of the post.

The wagon is positioned under the big hay door in the back of the barn. Peter is unhitched and led out front. I am lifted over the wire fence and told to stay there out of harm's way. I watch with fascination as the huge fork comes speeding out of the hayloft and digs far into the load. Out front, Carol has hitched Peter to the end of the rope that runs all the way from the fork, across the track in the loft and down to his harness. On top of the load, Uncle John drives the fork as deep as it will go and sets the teeth on either side. The shout is given: "G'head!" The great bundle of hay rides up the side of the barn and disappears into the loft where someone trips the teeth and the hay tumbles down in a heap to be spread evenly across the floor. There is a lot of dust and heat and frequent trips to the pump to get drinks of water.

Another shout and Carol releases Peter from the rope which disappears into the loft to ready the fork for the next load. Forkful after forkful disappears into the darkness of the loft until the truck wagon is almost empty. Uncle John surveys the hay still left.

"D'you think we can get that last in with the fork?" asks Grandpa.

"We can try," says Uncle John. He drives the fork less deeply, but a little too deeply, into the mound of hay that's left and shouts: "G'head!" Slowly the bundle of hay, wagon, and Uncle John rise up the side of the barn. Shouting and commotion ensue. "Back! Back!" Uncle John is shocked into speechlessness. He's suspended half way to the loft door, too low to climb in and too high to jump to the ground. Someone runs out front to back up Peter and after a tense few minutes the wagon slowly descends. An accident averted.

Walking Down the Lane

We have a lovely walk behind our house. It's only a farm lane, rutted and overgrown with grass and weeds, but it is bordered by fields on one side and spruce woods on the other. The tops of the trees are used by crows and ravens for lookout stations and are so even in height that they look as if they've been buzz cut by a barber.

Foxes and coyotes live there. The foxes are indigenous, some red, and a few silver ones that were released from dying fox farms in the decline of the fur trade many years ago. The coyotes are off-islanders, unwelcome intruders from the mainland that have come across on the winter ice. Their excuse is loss of habitat and they are not a bit gracious about it. Neighbourhood cats have gone missing, never to be seen again. These beasties don't come near here as the neighbours have dogs and they don't get along with dogs. Longstanding family feud, I guess. I haven't heard the coyotes lately. In the fall they sing on the far side of the field but I didn't hear them last fall. Maybe they've moved on.

We snowshoe back there in the winter. The fields stretch so white and sparkly in the winter sun. The squirrels chatter in the spruce trees and dislodge small cascades of snow here and there but we never see them. If you stand still and listen, there's a whisper to the silence. Perhaps it is the breathing of the forest and of life.

Marvin

He's a white kitty of indeterminate age. He lives in the barn next door. Of course, he hasn't always lived there, but he's lucky he's there now. He is currently one down on his allotment of nine lives and intends to keep it that way.

His story goes something like this. He was a kitty who belonged to a family with children. One day he had the misjudgment of biting one of them. No doubt he was provoked beyond endurance but we don't know about that part of the story. Momma said: "We can't harbour a cat who bites. He has to go to the shelter."

So Marvin was boxed up and carted off to the to the shelter to await his fate. No one wanted a cat who might bite. Marvin was down to his last day, in fact his last hours, when our kindly neighbour stopped by, looking for a kitty just like Marvin. She is also very fond of white kitties.

"You don't mind if he lives in the barn?" she asked.

"Oh, no," said the shelter ladies. "He bites."

"That won't matter," said the kindly neighbour, and took him home.

Marvin thought he was in Kitty Heaven.

A whole barn to himself and lots of mice to play with, although the mouse population seems depleted these days. He is treated to fresh food and water every day by the kindly neighbour. He never leaves the loft and daily surveys his kingdom from the loft doors that open onto a vista of fields and forest and all manner of wildlife.

SMALL HALLS

There is an ambiance to small halls that is not found anywhere else. The Clyde River Community Centre is such a place. In its original form it functioned as a two room schoolhouse, and although it has been repainted, re-carpeted and otherwise re-purposed, it still carries the sense of being a little out of time. A time no longer with us.

I remember such halls from my childhood and except for the daylight streaming in, there is an aura of church about them. I don't know why. Perhaps it is because we behaved differently then than we do now in our need to be independent and self-sufficient. The pleasant neighbourliness so essential to community is still present. Everyone visits with everyone before the program, enquiring about health and family and missing members and other public information. Everyone knows everyone and the crowd is mostly elderly. There is a lovely sense of continuity of community, everyone having known each other practically since the cradle. At the same time, strangers are welcomed. Of course, you have to give your pedigree to really pass muster. Fortunately I have one of sorts, my parents being Islanders. It is, after all, important to know where everyone fits and if you're related. I think we're probably all related here if we look back a generation or two.

The speaker on this occasion was Catherine Hennessey. She does historical research for enjoyment and to keep her mind active, so she says. I think perhaps there's more to it than that but she doesn't say. Today she speaks about Samuel Holland, the man who surveyed the Island in the 17th century. He did it for the crown and as a means of distributing land. He divided it into lots, parishes and then into farms of so many acres. Each lot was remarkably uniform in size except for a few where he had to fudge a little to make it come out as near to equal as he could. It was quite a feat, given that the Island is a little bow tie of a place with many coves and inlets. It's much narrower in the middle than at either end. He designated counties, and county towns and named parishes and places, most after one or another of his benefactors in Europe. The lot system is gone now but we mostly all know which lot we're from and who our founders were in each family and where they came from in the old country. This is kept alive by the practice of enquiring after pedigree. We all know where we fit.

After talks such as these there is always a lunch. Just a bite to eat, not a noontime spread, but a little something to warm your way home. There are sandwiches and fruit squares, brownies and cook-ies. The tea has a distinct flavour found only in small halls and at church teas. It is robust without being too strong, with an almost smoky taste. It does not vary from place to place, even across the wider Maritimes. I went to a church tea on Port Hood Island in Cape Breton a number of years ago and the tea was recognizable. The atmosphere was the same too, come to think of it. I've often wondered about this tea and tried many times to replicate it in my own kitchen but have not been successful. I wonder if it is the good well water without all the added chemicals, or the pot with its cellular memory of the many brewings in it despite being cleaned after every use. Perhaps it is the magic of the Scottish touch.

Harbour Hippo

We went for a ride on the Harbour Hippo yesterday. It's a clunky-looking vessel with enormous tires on land. The body is painted in combinations of blues and greens. Truly a curious vehicle. They took us for a ride around town at first, showing us historic buildings and telling the history and interesting anecdotes about each one. For example, in Fanningbank, the Lieutenant Governor's mansion, there is a bedroom set aside just for Royal visits. The Queen has stayed there several times. I rather delighted in the story of the little boy with a tour group, who decided that it might be fun to jump on the Queen's bed until a guard stopped him. He's probably the only child in the world outside of the Royal Family who has ever jumped on the Queen's bed. When Prince Charles and Camilla were here overnight this May they were not allowed to stay there for security reasons. One wonders why. Dangerous times in the Maritimes perhaps? Hard to believe. After all, this is Canada, and PEI is probably the safest province.

Eventually we circled back to the harbour and had a rather bumpy entry into the water. I was a little uneasy and reassured myself that we would never sink because of the oversized tires. We didn't, and continued out into the deeper harbour. We saw ungainly black birds somewhat resembling pelicans that were identified as cormorants. They nest on the remains of the old bridge pilings. There were plenty of seagulls and we even saw a seal. Our guide mentioned that fishermen put down their lobster pots in the harbour. These are baited and the cormorants are such good divers they would go to the bottom and steal the bait from the pots. Our guide told us that Charlottetown Harbour was the cleanest harbour in Canada. We also have two kinds of jelly fish, white ones and red ones. The red ones are the ones that sting.

It was interesting looking at familiar things from a different angle. From the water it's kind of hard to tell exactly where I am. Everything is farther to the right or left than I think it should be, and I've got a good sense of direction. There were a lot of sail boats out today. There was a breeze and it was sort of cloudy, just the right kind of weather to enjoy the water. I'm very fair skinned and always manage to get burnt somewhere despite gallons of sunscreen. I remember once being on Chesapeake Bay and coming home with a line of red vee's across my hairline in front, where I'd missed with the sunscreen application.

After a tour around the Charlottetown Harbour

we returned to dry land. Our guide treated us to suckers on the way in. Mine was grape. It has been a very long time since I've even thought of the joy of a sweet sucker.

Fiberglas Horses

I like to look at horses. I don't ride and have no desire to, I just like to look. There was a beautiful honey-coloured horse with a creamy mane and tail who used to live in the field behind our house. I looked for him the first thing every morning and watched him off and on all day. He was a handsome fellow by the name of Aksa. His original name was Hacksaw. It was a highly unsuitable name for such a beautiful animal so his owner renamed him Aksa. Much better, in my opinion. He lives elsewhere now and I miss him. He essentially made my day.

I have ridden a few times in my life when I was much younger but I don't think I would do it now. They are very tall beasties and rather intimidating. I remember one trail ride I was on that turned out with the horse doing whatever he wanted to while I held on for dear life. We were crossing a stream and my mount, usually a lumbering old thing who plodded from point A to point B, decided he wanted a drink. Nothing would change his mind. Down went his head and he slurped to his heart's content despite my best effort to get his head up. The trail ride leader kept yelling: "Get his head up!" I tugged hard on the reins to no avail. Finally she came riding up along side of me, grabbed his bridle and with a hearty heave succeeded in raising his head and persuading him out of the stream. That was my last horseback ride many years ago.

There's a much more manageable horse just down the road. He patiently stands with his right front leg raised as if to pull the buggy full of plastic flowers harnessed on behind. I'm not sure where he's going but I guess he's undecided too as he hasn't moved for at least three years. He lost that raised front leg to the snowplow last winter but he bravely stood on three legs until the snow-bank melted this spring. Lately he went through reconstructive surgery and his leg is restored, and his flowers are refreshed for another season.

Inside the Box

I remember the day my bagpipes came. It was in the fall. The day was sunny and the leaves were turning. I think it may have been October because it wasn't raining. Any later in the year it would have been raining or snowing. The Maritimes are like that, November being a dark and rainy month. Despite its only being thirty days it seems much longer because of the oppressive darkness and rain.

I went down to the customs office, out of the sunshine into a dark and cheerless basement. I had ordered my bagpipes about eight weeks before. They came by surface mail in a boat across the ocean from Scotland. Eight long weeks of waiting. At last they were here. I carried them home under my arm dreaming of the parades and concerts in which I would join the other pipers.

That evening I call the Pipe Major, and he came right over. The bagpipes needed seasoning and possibly even tying in. I don't remember that part. The bag may have already been tied to the drone stocks at the factory. It requires strong hands and lots of tying in cord to accomplish that. I was shown how to melt the seasoning in its can in a pan of water on the stove, then to pour it carefully into the chanter stock and to rub it around all the seams and into the base of the stocks. This keeps it air tight.

We inserted the reeds in the appropriate drones and the drones to their appropriate stocks. We attached the beautiful white pipe chords with the fancy tassels on the ends and added the flowing pipe ribbons. These cords hold the drones the proper distance apart and keep them from falling off your shoulder when you play. The ribbons are just for decoration and to signify who you play with or what clan you're from according to the tartan they're made of.

They were complete. The Pipey picked them up, chewed a little on the leather flap inside the blowpipe to make it flexible and capable of keeping the air in the bag. He tucked it under his arm and blew into it. The bag filled to a great belly of air. He chorded the chanter and tuned the drones and played a tune. Oh, the joy of hearing my own bagpipes played for the first time! What skill I had to aspire to. It took many months of hard practice to even be able to blow a full set of drones, but that's another story.

The Care and Feeding of Bagpipes

What do pipers wear under their kilts? This is a question that has been a puzzle to some non-pipers for many years. I know for a fact that Kenny wears Fruit of the Looms. We had a brief glance at his briefs when he tripped and fell on the lawn in front of the University of Prince Edward Island. I've heard it said that Kent goes "regimental." My friend Karen found out quite by accident one windy day on parade. He didn't have weights in the hem of his kilt and a fresh breeze from the Northumberland Strait put a tilt in his kilt that he wasn't expecting. Of course, Kent never expected much of anything anyway, his mind was always wandering on to things much higher than his hemline.

All this aside, playing bagpipes is an exhilarating pastime. It's a satisfying hobby and one that you can share with all the neighbours. It requires a certain finger dexterity and a strong body. Non-pipers think that it takes good lungs to blow a set of pipes. This is a myth. What it takes is a good diaphragm and a lot of perseverance. Several months of daily blowing are required to build up the diaphragm, rib, and lip muscles to the point at which you are ready to march in a parade.

A parade is a whole different experience. It has hills and potholes on its route, and lots of people along the curb who expect pipe bands to play constantly. There are horses too. The Parade Marshall always sees fit to put the horses in front of the pipe bands. It keeps the horses moving, and improves the footwork of the pipers. I've tiptoed round many a bouquet of "tulips" in my day!

Taking care of a set of bagpipes is like taking care of a baby. They must be dressed appropriately in a tartan or black velvet bag cover with matching or contrasting trim. They cough and burp when you least expect it, and they must be fed on special formula. The formula is called seasoning, and in the old days pipers made their own. Each piper had his own recipe which may or may not have contained a generous portion of Highland Whiskey, as well as certain oils or mutton fat, and either honey or molasses. The rest of the ingredients were as variable as the pipers. It was never safe for them to lay the instruments on the ground because the ants would mistake them for a picnic.

Nowadays, the seasoning is commercially prepared according to a special formula, and what goes into each brand remains a mystery. The list of ingredients in chemical form on the labels is incomprehensible to your average piper and could very well be only mutton fat, molasses, and whiskey. Only a chemist would know for sure. It comes in a red tartan can with a thistle on the label and requires heating in a water bath on the stove until it becomes liquid.

A few years ago a manufacturer of pipe seasoning created a type that would remain in liquid form and would not require heating. It was a great boon to those of us who believed that bagpipes should be self-servicing. When it came time to season the bag, I dutifully performed the task with the liquid preparation. The only difference in the procedure between the liquid and solid kind was that I had to hang the pipes up for an hour or so to drain the excess. This pipe seasoning was a cloudy beige liquid when I poured it into the bag. When it came out it was distinctly orange. I hung the bag from the door of the kitchen cabinet, sat a glass underneath to catch the drip, and went off about my business. Awhile later I returned and took down the pipes, leaving the glass of orange coloured seasoning on the counter. I didn't know what else to do with it since I could neither put it back in the bottle nor put it down the drain.

It is the habit in my parents' household to have a bedtime snack. My father, my mother and my sister retired to the kitchen at the appointed hour. My mother's motto in life is: "Waste not, want not."

She mistook the glass of seasoning for orange juice and took two big swigs of it before she realized what it was. Everyone was horrified, and my sister began reading the ingredient list and the various virtues of this concoction. "It cleans and seals all the seams and pores," she read aloud. "It disinfects. It retains its pleasant odour. It is good for preserving the life of old bags." Glances were exchanged between my father and my sister, and they tried unsuccessfully to keep straight faces. My sister giggled and my father began to laugh. My mother said: "Humph! Margaret Anne had better be more careful where she leaves that stuff!" It was several years before I could gather the courage to ask her if she'd had any ill effects from the experience. "No," she snorted,"I never even got a good burp from it!"

THE WRITING LIFE

JUST IMAGINE!

Imagination is as much a thief of time as procrastination. The difference is that imagination gives you something wonderful to show for the time it steals, while the time stolen by procrastination is merely wasted and gone forever. I discovered this wonderful secret some years ago when I took a creative writing class. I had always wanted to study creative writing, and when opportunity tapped gently on my academic door, I opened to it.

All that semester I worked at writing poems, scenes from different points of view, snippets of dialogue around a particular theme, more poems, and two short stories. The first glimmer of awareness that I could actually write came when I got an A for a poem. The process began to be fun rather than work, and by the end of the course I was having more fun than I'd had in a long time.

It was exciting! My imagination, that I'd thought to be non-existent, was suddenly alive and bursting with ideas and associations. I regretted the end of the class. I felt rootless and dissatisfied. I moped. My temper was uncertain. In short, I missed writing. One afternoon while I waited for my husband to give a final exam I noticed that his computer was on and I began playing with it. I wondered how long I could keep a dialogue going without running out of something to say, and having nothing better to do since I had no exams to study for, I began a dialogue between an old lady in a nursing home and her best friend who was already a ghost. This was a tricky proposition because the old lady, being a stroke victim, couldn't talk sense. It was fun. I did it again the next day, and the day after that, and then again the day after that, until I had thirty pages of dialogue, several other characters on both sides of the veil, a hero and a heroine, and most of the details of a plot worked out. I felt a tickle of excitement in my tummy. I hardly dare voice the words to John when he asked, "I think I'm writing a novel!"

I continued working every day all morning for six weeks. I had no idea how to chapter, nor how to end a scene. I just wrote my heart out. In the end, after revisions of a sort I had a novel of 269 pages. It's a good story even yet, but now after the birth of six more novels I see its flaws. They are problems which, I see now, can easily be solved.

Over the following years I have not only learned a lot about writing, I have also learned a lot about imagination. It's almost like a living thing. I have discovered that I must not overwork it. It gets tired and needs a rest just as I do. I have found that I must give it adequate time to do its thinking and planning for me. If I try to force it, it will balk and nothing will happen. It needs to be fed. I must offer for its delectation the daily events and minutiae of life. Imagination is insatiable in some ways and accepts for processing everything I might offer. All morsels of information are taken into my subconscious to be digested, and when the bits come out again they are part of something different and are so transformed that the owners of the original bits will never recognize them as their own.

That semester I learned to journal and it has become another of the ways I feed my imagination. Journaling is not just keeping a diary, although it does have aspects of a diary in that if it is being properly kept, the writing will be daily. What journaling does is help me to organize my thoughts and ideas, note observations I've made about people, places, and events that have important content concerning things which I have been thinking about. In the long term it helps me to see my growth as a person and as a writer. It also keeps track of the important events in my life because I do use it as a diary as well. Journaling also keeps the creative flow going when I'm not working on any particular project. The old saying that "eating makes appetite" can be adapted here to describe writing. The more I write, the more I want to write, and journaling is the bridge between projects.

I feed my imagination by reading. I am a voracious reader, especially in science. I read everything within reach and if I have nothing else to read, I read the labels on the ketchup bottle. I play with words. I try to discover how many words I can make out of just one word by rearranging the letters. I juxtapose words that normally would not be used together. I do crossword puzzles, the harder the better. I read other writers' novels and spin my own ideas from them. I create scenes in my head. I picture the scientists whom I read about, white-coated, in front of their microscopes, making important discoveries. I wonder what they're like to live with, if they're married, whether they have children, do they have pets, and do they get along with their mothers-in-law? All this reading and wondering and juxtaposing feeds my imagination.

Imagination needs exercise. It can become very lazy if it's not exercised regularly. Free association is a workout for the imagination. Like walking, it doesn't require any special equipment beyond what I was born with. It can be done anywhere and no one knows I'm doing it, except perhaps my husband. Something in my environment will catch my attention and I'm off and running with a series of "what if's ," and "I wonder why's," and suddenly I'm making some of the most preposterous connections between improbable people, places and things. Nothing needs to make sense when I'm free associating, but a crazy kind of sense occurs and leads me to ideas for stories and funny anecdotes. I am reminded of other things I've seen and heard in a different context, and a new door in my perception is opened and a whole new adventure begins.

Nurturing an imagination takes time and effort but it repays a hundred-fold in the long run. I never worry about writers' block because I know that with an appropriate stimulus I can let my imagination go and free associate anything my heart desires. I set the writing problem for the day consistent with the story I'm spinning and let go. I write everything that comes to my mind within the context of my story, no matter what it is. I refrain from passing judgment on anything my imagination dictates to me. That will come later. That's what revisions are for.

Keeping an imagination is a little like keeping a cat. It has a secret life all its own, but if I take time to properly train and feed it, it will come whenever I call. To free associate a little further, imagination has elements of the cat burglar who was called the kissing bandit. The burglar would steal the ladies' jewels and reward them with a kiss. Imagination steals my time but it leaves me with such a sweet reward.

Writing by the Seat of my Pants

When I was taking the Masters' Degree in English at the University of Missouri at Kansas City, I was taught the germ theory of writing. You hear a story or read an article in a magazine and take a word or a phrase from it and create your own story around it. It need only be a word or two, something that triggers your imagination and sends it off into the wilds of your creative mind. As long as you take the idea and don't repeat it word for word, you can go where you will with it. It is only something to spark your creativity. You can separate the idea completely from its source once you get going on your project because it will have no relationship to its origin anymore and is probably no longer even recognizable as coming from there.

I get my stories from my elders. They're all great story-tellers. *Anna's Secret* is a case in point. The story is based on the story of Anne Beaton's hollow where a murder took place 150 years ago that was blamed on an ancestor of mine. He was subsequently cleared of the deed and left Prince Edward Island. I took the fact of her murder and fictionalized it by changing her personality, the circumstances surrounding her life and death, and putting in characters who never existed outside of my imagination. I asked myself questions like: What if she had been someone entirely different than who she was purported to be? Who was she really? Who did she really go to see? Was it an innocent visit or was it a clandestine affair as everyone thought? Who really murdered her? What were the motivations? Questions of this nature led to a well fleshed-out novel not based on the original story, which was probably based in truth. Then I took the original question of who she really was and who I thought she should be, and dug and explored all her fictional relationships, which eventually led to the dénouement.

I have never used an outline. I tried it once because I was told it was the best way to work but it didn't work for me. It kept me too bound by the structure of the outline. I felt I had to write by the rules when my characters wanted to do something different. I had to let them be themselves. They become living people in my mind and you have to let people do whatever it is they need to do. They talk to me and argue with me and agree with me just like real people. You can't be too controlling or your story will become too rigid and awkward. Let your characters tell the story. Keep notes as to who is related to whom and when they did a certain thing and anything else you think you might get hazy on as the story moves along. That way you don't have to keep going back to look for it, should you need that information again. So try writing without an outline, you never know where your characters will take you or why they want you to go there.

On Cue

I have on hand a book that is valuable to me. It is called *The Writer's Book of Days* by Judy Reeves, published by New World Library in 1999. It is a book of writing prompts and I have used it extensively. It gives me focus and something to work with. There is a topic for every day of the year. Not only have I written a goodly number of short essays but also a few poems from the work.

One such prompt was "write about a purchase." What kind of purchase? I asked myself. The Louisiana Purchase? Seward's Folly? None of the above? I decided to begin free-writing and came up with this short essay:

It's interesting how differently people approach shopping. When I was in Minneapolis this summer, a momentary acquaintance and I went to the Great Mall. Now I know the meaning of "shop 'til you drop." I didn't buy much but it was fun to watch Terese. Everything went on the credit card, and the gaudier her purchases were, the better. We had fun. This was where I bought *The Writer's Book of Days*.

The second most important thing was a harmonica. I had always wanted one but I could never justify spending the money. It's interesting how being away from home and under the influence of another shopper can change our perceptions. They were on sale too, so that made it okay, and I actually learned to play coherent, recognizable tunes. We spent the whole day at the mall and Terese bought lots of jewellery—a pendant watch encrusted with fake coral, blue shoes and large clip-on earrings. On she went buying whatever caught her fancy, with a short stop for lunch. I bought a pair of very circumspect earrings.

Normally I'm a very efficient shopper. I shop with a mental list and only go spring and fall when the sales are on. For me to spend all day at a mall is unheard of. You can hardly get me in the doors. I'm reluctant to part with my cash and don't respond well to pushy sales people. I'll never make a dropper shopper.

Once when I was still nursing I startled a colleague and myself by going from a simple nursing procedure to mining minerals on Mars in ten easy steps. My colleague just looked at me in wonder and said: "I don't know how you do that."

In fact, it's quite easy. The trick is to relax and let your mind run with the topic. For example, this is where I went with the prompt from Ms. Reeves' book titled "Saving the Night."

The night won't save anyone. This I know. It doesn't cover anything up very well. It's not even particularly safe in your own bed with all those creepy little aliens running around carving up cattle and impregnating women. I wonder what the babies look like? Would it have the alien's hair? Uncle Bob's nose? Aunt Gertie's teeth and a personality like a dead fish? Crossing two species is not a safe bet. Why would the aliens want to crossbreed with us anyway? They would only lose their civility and become belligerant and war prone like we are. Goodness knows, being human is difficult enough without adding alien propensities into the mix. So if you ever see a short human with grey skin, give him a wide berth.

Another night-themed prompt was: "The Darkness Proposes." It took a different direction, more earthly than other-worldly. It goes like this:

The darkness doesn't propose a thing. It's what we read into it that gives it a bad reputation. Who hasn't dreamed of their first kiss and where it might take place? It certainly wouldn't take place in broad daylight. How dreadful that someone might see that first awkward peck of the swoop-kiss of the determined suitor. So the safest place to try is in the dark, away from porch lights and prying parents.

Night was only the beginning. For some perhaps the ending. And away I go again. Thoughts and ideas line up in my head all clamoring to be heard at once. It's amazing where your mind will take you if you let it. From saving the night to aliens to first kisses is quite a leap and I got there by slides and leaps and sidesteps. Of course, I wasn't watching where I was going so I could have gone anywhere with the idea. Such is the power of the prompt.

Book Signings

Book signings are so much fun. I really enjoy talking to people who stop by to enquire about my books. They seem very curious about where I get my ideas and how I develop them. Another question that frequently arises is, are my characters anyone real? I explain that they are composites of the many people I have met over my lifetime—a characteristic here, a quirk of personality there. In a way it's like baking a fruitcake, a few pieces of fruit here, a few nuts there, some spices for interest and some batter to hold it all together. Besides, I don't want to insult or embarrass anyone who might still be alive to complain.

I hear the best stories from people, triggered mostly by my Partners Paranormal series. The stories are purely imaginary on my part but the whole idea seems to stimulate the telling of other peoples' experiences in the paranormal realms. Haunted stories abound among those of us who are of Scottish or Irish descent. Everyone wants to tell me theirs. I'm grateful because sometimes those are the quirkiest and richest stories in terms of content. More hooks to hang my imaginary adventures on. I guess I must be a receptive listener although I usually keep my own ghost encounters very quiet.

I'm glad that people want to tell me their stories. It is stories that keep society together and connected. "D'you remember the time we … ?" And away they go and apply more glue to their shared origins. If you know the stories, you are part of the crowd, and will always be part of the crowd. If you don't know the stories, you can only ever be on the periphery.

THEM DRY BONES

Triggers for my poem, "Dry Bones," did not begin with bones. I was thinking about some of the aspects of living on a sandstone and clay island. My thoughts turned specifically to the topic of erosion, and how much land we lose each year due to weather and sea forces.

There are several seaside cemeteries that have lost so much land that they are discharging their tenants into the sea one by one. The wood in the coffins is still buoyant and they go bobbing off to points unknown on other coasts.

Then I thought: What if the bones were still sentient? What would they think of their little cruise? Now, I know, in reality as we understand it, that bones never have been aware and think-ing, but just imagine for a moment if they were. Would they enjoy the adventure or would they be appalled and upset about being so rudely awakened and thrust into the cold North Atlantic Ocean, even if it was in the summer?

As I was writing this poem all I could hear in my mind's ear was the song, "Them bones, them bones, them dry bones." The poem, published in *Pathways*, is the product of my free association.

Snow Wraiths

What strange things catch my attention to write poetry about. The events are usually small and insignificant as in the poem "Snow Wraiths."

I was driving home at dusk and there was a skiff of snow on the ground. The wind picked it up over the tops of hills and whirled it just so to make what looked like people. Around and around they danced according to the will of the wind. Sometimes they looked like figures of long dead friends and relatives. The resemblances were sometimes so close I could have named them. I wonder if their spirits really did inhabit the snow whirls, if only briefly, or would they be horrified to even think such a thing could happen? Some of them were quite religious and, unless they had changed in the meantime, they would probably be appalled. Of course, dancing in the snow might be very freeing. Never having tried it, I wouldn't know.

READING FOR THE LOVE OF IT

I have always loved books. I'm not sure but that I was born with a book in my hand. I would wait for Dad to come home from work and come running with my book for him to read to me. It was a great frustration to me that I couldn't read for myself, and I listened to my story books over and over until I had them memorized and could follow along as if I really were reading. "Daddy, what's that word there?" was a constant refrain.

The first time I figured out a word all by myself was in kindergarten We sat at little tables with chairs, two children to a table. My table happened to be beside the side blackboard and there were words written on the blackboard from another class. I stared and stared at the word, sounding it out in my mind until suddenly I knew! The word was "surprise." It was as if a veil had been lifted, snatched away, really, and I have never stopped reading since.

As a child, I read everything I could lay my hands on. I joined the library when I was six, taking out four books every two weeks. I remember the very first book I ever borrrowed. It was about animals and the chapter I most remember was the one on Stickleback fish. It fascinated me that the father Stickleback cared for the young fish.

Over the years I borrowed books from my school friends and returned them after several readings. Sometimes I would read a book cover to cover and when I had finished, I would turn it over and start all over again. I still reread books. I have six bookcases filled to the brim and will need another one very soon. I have books stacked everywhere. Of course, my taste in reading material has changed over the years. Nowadays I am more apt to read philosophy, science or religion than a romance, but if a good romance comes along, I'll read that too. I love poetry. I think that Emily Dickinson, Keats and Robbie Burns are probably my favourites. Books have been my friends through thick and thin and I feel out of sorts if I can't take time to read.

My father encouraged my love of reading. He was a carpenter, a real craftsman. The work of his hands will endure long after I'm gone and probably the rest of the descendents too. The basement always smelled of wood and sawdust. He did contract work for homeowners: roofs, cupboards, bookcases, and any thing that required the use of wood. If he didn't know how to make a thing he'd figure it out. He designed my jewellery box right down to the little drawer in the bottom. I treasure it. He had a little stove made out of a barrel in the basement where he used to burn scraps of lumber left over from his projects. It would be a violation of the insurance policy nowadays, I'm sure.

He had a great respect for education and was a great reader. As a consequence, all his children went on to college. I remember him reading poetry aloud in the evening. He always read from *The Book of Popular Verse*. One night he was reading *The Ballad of Sam McGee*. I was playing on the floor and he didn't think I was listening. He got to the part about warming old Sam up in the boiler of the iced-in freighter and Sam woke up from his frozen state and said: "Please close the door. Since I left Plum Tree down in Tennesee, it's the first time I've been warm." I began to laugh and Dad realized I had been listening and that I'd gotten the joke. I was about seven or eight years old and to this day I remember passages from that particular poem.

Dad's been gone now for some years. He left us with a great legacy, a solid education, a good sense of values and proper behaviour and enquiring minds. Because of his example I have never stopped reading and learning and figuring things out. He was never very talkative but I sometimes wish he were still here so I could run some ideas past him just to hear what he would say.

Two Hundred Poems

I can hardly believe that I now have over two hundred poems on paper. I never realized that I had so much to say. I've learned a lot. One thing is that if I have something to say I'd better say it clearly. I know from reading poetry that the ones I most enjoy are the ones that say what they mean. Poetry should be multilayered but not obscure. One way to make sure that you are speaking clearly on your topic is to use adequate punctuation. You don't need a lot, just periods at the ends of sentences and a well-placed comma here and there. It gives your reader something to hang onto when they start diving into the depths of the work. Something to come back to when they go too far astray. What did I really mean? This or that? Without punctuation the impact of the work is lessened. I always think that if it's important enough to put on paper, it's worth doing it well.

Memories

What are your earliest memories? Most people can't remember back before four years of age, a few to three. What they do remember is fragmented; snapshots at best. On the other hand, I remember specific events from when I was about ten months old. Some scenes have me still in the crib in the dining room, and in diapers.

I started walking when I was ten or so months old. We had just moved into our new house and things were still in boxes. My mother's two sisters came to visit, and see the new house and the new niece. I remember them standing in the hallway and mother introducing them to me. What are "ants" I wondered. Then I turned and toddled down the hall and sat down, plunk, on my diapered bottom as toddlers do. I was beside a cardboard box and the side of the box was up to my shoulder. There are a number of remembrances of this nature.

What is the purpose of these early memories? For me, they add depth and meaning to my early life. A place to start from. And now, fodder for my novels should I ever need it. They provide me with insight into being a toddler and a very young child. For example: Roddy, the young boy in the Partners Paranormal series. He's three when we first meet him. He is precocious and quite charming, if I do say so myself. He knows things beyond his years, but not necessarily their significance. We almost have to interact with him as if he were a little adult.

For me this is the importance of early memories. They lead us to our sense of self, and for me, to a sense of who my characters are as individuals. I seem to have a thread of character that has not changed from when I was first aware of being a person. I have certainly grown and learned over the years but there is always the foundational sense of being me that has not changed even after all these years.

CARCASSES

I was grumbling to John this morning about how every topic I think of for a poem seems to have been done to death by greater and lesser poets than I. He told me about the view of a professor he once had regarding research topics. The professor said not to look at the topic in hand as a carcass with all the meat picked off. Every researcher's view is a fresh look at the overall subject with connections to be made and new ideas to be proposed. The subject eventually gets honed to its pristine point and we are able to see our way forward with sure steps.

So where does that leave me? I still don't have a topic. No focus, no poem, so to speak. I suppose I could write on carcasses, but nothing grabs me there either. When I write I like to know where I'm starting from and where the end is located. The middle generally takes care of itself. The trick is to get back far enough mentally to see the whole picture. Then the carcass becomes clear in its entirety and I can imagine it in different styles of dress.

Tools of the Trade

My fountain pen is old now. It is navy blue with marbling. The clasp is gone. Not that the absence of the clasp is of much notice as I don't wear it on my person anyway. I sometimes think the nib is getting sharp from use. I don't want to get another one. This one fits my hand. It's like holding hands with a beloved. I do most of my hand writing with it. My journal has been written with it ever since I bought it twenty years ago. I sometimes wonder how many gallons of ink I've run through over the years. If I could measure distress in gallons of ink I'd have gone through buckets of it. Fifteen years of our time together have been brutal. Before that it wasn't much better, but I didn't have my trusty fountain pen.

Many poems, blogs and essays have been written with this pen. I tried my hand at writing a Tanka this morning. The subject came up in the writing group this week. I don't usually like writing in forms. If I have something to say in a poem I like to tell it as I see it and not spend my time fighting with lines of a certain number of syllables. One of our members brought a couple of Tankas to the group, which got me thinking that I should try one. Hers were good; mine needs some work yet. I tried Haiku once. I came to the conclusion that you needed more skill than I had to create them and unless you were really good, the poem was pretty awful. All that wrestling with form seemed such a waste of time and I never did manage to say what I meant. I don't like to fight with rhyme either. I can rhyme pretty well but I still don't seem to say what I mean and they come out sounding like limericks. My big thing is rhythm. As a musician, my ear hears rhythms in words. My poems always seem to turn themselves into little melodies in my head.

Through it all I have my fountain pen. I write poetry and essays by hand and my pen gives them the right amount of boldness in their expression. I can scratch out lines and eliminate words, write above the original in the space. I feel as if there is power and strength in my pen that I wouldn't have otherwise. The paste that passes for ink in a ballpoint pen fades much too quickly and in time my words disappear back to where they came from, wherever that is located.

Mothers Everywhere

Like it or not, they're ours to keep. Never having been a mother except to kitties, I can only speak from observation. I understand the job is difficult from start to finish; if it is ever finished. I've learned a lot from my friends and neighbours about mothering, most of it good, some of it not so much. Of course, being childless by circumstance gives me a unique point of view. If I had ever become a mother I would probably have done things differently then than I think I would do now.

When I taught piano I had little girl who expected a sticker even when she hadn't done any work. She never gained a sense of achievement, only a sense of entitlement. Granted, it was only a sticker and I certainly had plenty and didn't begrudge her, but there was no incentive to better herself. This occurred years ago. I wonder where she went and what she did with her life. She'd be nearly thirty by now.

You can guess by this story that I think that follow-through and legitimate achievement are an important element to teach children so that they can become successful adults.

Easier said than done? Probably.

Mothers are everywhere. I didn't realize that I wrote so much about mothers. They are usually a little peripheral to the central story but still have great influence on the female protagonists. For instance, *Mattie's Story*. Mattie's mother was gruff and rather short in her replies to Mattie and her questions. Her words lived on in Mattie even after she left home. She was ultra responsible as a new wife, for example, the episode of the rancid butter and the grease ants. As a potential mother she was very protective of her unborn child, for example, the scene where David unthinkingly takes them sliding over the roof of the house just because the snow was deep enough and the sleighing was fun.

On the other hand, her friend Cora, whose mother was almost absentee because of her "condition," had no compunction about looking for her "fun" with never a thought for the consequences. It nearly cost her her reputation.

In *Shades of Molly*, Gertrude did her best for her mother while realizing her short-comings and loving her anyway. Her mother fancied herself a seer and Gertrude suffered the consequences all of her childhood and, as an adult, did her best to distance herself from the "gift," nearly missing her true calling. In the sequel *Ghost Baby*, she has a child of her own and brings him up entirely differently.

Anna's Secret is different again. Anna has a special relationship with her only child that is misunderstood by everyone, including his father. She has a rather different relationship with neighbours and friends, and again is misunderstood. When the truth about Anna comes out it reveals a unique story.

It was recently brought to my attention that my stories all revolve around pregnancy, birthing and motherhood, either by delivery or adoption. Having been a nurse I've been at a few deliveries and I am always in awe of the process. The care that goes into carrying an infant to term and then the effort of a healthy delivery just amazes me. When I think of what I know now, and what my characters knew then about child bearing is, in some ways, worlds apart. The mishaps that led to stillbirths and miscarriages then that don't happen now, for example Jean, a character in *Anna's Secret,* and all her miscarriages and how it led to the disaster that was Anna's secret to bear. Then there are the deformities and weaknesses that children were born with. I'm thinking in particular of Duncan and Hector and their simple, silly ways, and Mattie's mother's infant who was born with a cast in her eye, a congenital cataract, while Mattie's baby was born perfectly formed and sensible.

There are also the ideas that you have to

eat for two when you're expecting, that you must have a lengthy lying-in period around the actual delivery date, and the notion that if you saw a frightening or unpleasant sight your infant would be born "marked" with a scar or a birthmark in the shape of the frightening object. I, myself, was born with a birthmark in the shape of an airplane on my hip which has since disappeared. I wonder what that signifies?

So this is my expression of motherhood. They are composites of all the mothers I have known, maternal and otherwise. My experiences with mothers young and old have stood me in good stead as I weave the stories about my characters and observe them as they mature, through their experiences, into motherhood.

Following are two short stories I wrote on the theme of mothers and daughters.

Life Insurance

They buried my father today. My brother and I stood side by side in the slanting November rain enduring the penetrating wind straight off the winter grey Atlantic. Enduring also, the dull monotone of the priest reciting the committal service.

"From dust we came, unto dust we shall return," he mourned.

My clod of chilly wet earth bounced hollowly off the top of the coffin. It was followed in a moment by my brother's contribution. I stared hard into the coffin-sized hole in a vain effort to contain the warm tears which mixed with the rain and quickly cooled to November iciness. I cleared my throat roughly and my brother's arm tightened around my waist.

"Okay, Babe?" he whispered.

I swallowed hard against the spasm in my throat, then nodded. His use of my father's old pet name for me was almost my undoing. I was glad the others preferred comfort to convention and had returned to the house and the hot buffet which awaited them. I shivered as the rain increased and a particularly vicious gust of wind turned our umbrella inside out and finished its usefulness. My brother tossed its remains behind the next tombstone and we hunched our shoulders against the cold.

"Amen," intoned the priest, ending the service. The hem of his robe collected a rim of black as he moved around the open grave to offer his condolences. I watched in horror as his heavy tread dislodged the earth between the graves and a cascade of pebbles and clots of dirt rattled down onto my father's coffin. I imagined I saw my mother's coffin in the adjoining grave. The priest trod on, oblivious to the destruction he had left behind; oblivious, too, to the cascade of memories released in my mind.

"A fine man. I knew him as a boy," the priest was saying as he shook hands with my brother. I blinked at this remark. My father had turned ninety-three two weeks before he died. The priest was only forty. What could he possibly mean? I dragged my eyes away from the sight of my mother's coffin and focused my mind with difficulty. Father had been a member of this parish all of his life except for his four year stint in the navy during the war. Of course! Father McKinley was the tenth grandson of one of my mother's ancient friends. She was long since dead and buried in the next row. I grasped his extended hand and tried to smile.

"Your father always carried candy in his pocket for us boys," he said. "He used to make us sing for it and no matter how badly we sang we always got a piece. The only time I didn't get one was the first time when I was too shy to sing. He laughed and said that I hadn't earned it. The other boys all got one and I didn't, but I made sure I got one the next time. I practised all week for it." He smiled at the memory and seemed disposed to remain reminiscing from under the comfort of his umbrella for some time.

I shivered as a trickle of rain rolled off the brim of my hat and down the back of my neck. "That sounds just like Father." I clenched my teeth to keep them from chattering, and the need to shiver transferred itself to my body and I began to tremble.

"Let's go home, Babe," My brother's hand under my elbow urged me away.

The ride away from the cemetery was much quicker than the slow procession toward it. I guess we don't want to hasten the final trip of our dear departed! The thought flashed through my mind and almost jolted me into laughter. The laughter changed to melancholy as we rounded the corner and I saw the quiet street lined with cars.

I sighed. "I was hoping they'd all be gone."

"They'll be gone soon enough," observed my brother. "Most of them are at least as old as Father!"

With difficulty I controlled another urge to laugh as we entered the long living room. The parlour, my father had always called it, though its resemblance to a parlour was passing at best. The buffet had been set up in the adjoining dining room and people stood or sat around with little plates of sausages and quiches and cups of coffee. Mother's good china looked fragile in the palsied hands of her ancient friends. The catering staff scurried back and forth replenishing the table.

"Ah, here they are!" Mr. Brown set his plate down with a little crash on the mahogany side table. "You look like a pair of drowned rats," he said. My expression must have given me away for he apologized instantly. "Sorry! Poor choice of words! You'd better go and get dry. You'll catch your death of … " His voice trailed away. "Anyway, go get dry."

When we returned, the crowd was stirring restlessly. They've fed, I thought unpleasantly, now they're ready to go. I began my tour of the room.

"Mr. Edwards, so nice of you to come!"

"Yes, we've been friends for many years. He was a fine man. He'll be sorely missed. A pillar of the church."

He paid back what you snitched out of the collection plate and never said a word, I thought unkindly. "So kind of you to say so." I released his hand and moved on.

"Mr. and Mrs. MacMillan! I'm so pleased to see you." I was pleased to see them. Mrs. MacMillan had been like a second mother to me when I was a child. They had moved away twenty years ago to be near their son, so it had been a long time since I had seen them.

"We came just as soon as we heard, dear," said Mrs. MacMillan enfolding me in a warm hug. "I was ill when your dear mother passed away so we weren't able to come then."

"Yes, you wrote to me," I replied. "You're feeling better?"

"Oh, well, you know how it is, we're all getting older."

It was then that I noticed the walker folded beside her chair. "You're having trouble getting around now?"

"Ever since I broke my ankle last year." Her eyes followed my glance toward the walker. "It's kind of like my security blanket, you know."

"How's your brother?" asked Mr. MacMillan.

"He'll be along in a minute," I replied. "He's just checking on the caterers."

"Well, you two have certainly done well for yourselves. Your mother would be proud of you."

"Yes, I expect she would." But I'd never know it, I thought bitterly. The image of the cascade of stones and the edge of her casket flashed back into my mind, but I held the memories away from me.

"What exactly is it that you do for a living?" asked Mr. MacMillan.

"I was the editor-in-chief for *City Magazine*, but I'm retired now."

"Ah, yes, I remember your father telling me about that. You took that magazine from a local rag to a national glossy in a very short time, if I recall."

I smiled. "It took about six years. Once it reached a certain size and style and circulation, it almost took off on its own."

"And your brother. What's he doing now? He must be nearly ready to retire himself."

I glanced in my brother's direction. His cheeks had taken on a familiar flush. "Ah, no—not exactly. He's been on disability for a couple of years now."

"Really! Was he injured at work?" asked Mrs. MacMillan, all motherly concern.

"You might say that," I replied cautiously. "He fell down stairs on the way from a sales meeting. He injured his back." I didn't add that he'd had a liquid lunch with the client and if he hadn't fallen and been pensioned off, he'd have been let go.

"I see," said Mr. MacMillan. I looked at him inquiringly and saw that he really did see. "That's too bad. Such a disappointment."

"It was, indeed. Well, I must greet the others." I prepared to move on. "I can see they're anxious to leave." I drifted on to the next group and held out my hand to little Mr. Englund. He reached up and gave me a peck on the cheek. "So like your dear mother," he sighed.

I smiled at him. My mother would have had you for breakfast, I thought. "Now you always say that and it's not a bit true," I said.

"Oh, yes, more than you know," he insisted. "I remember her from the day she turned sixteen. My cousin dragged me to her birthday party. I went, but not very willingly, and when I saw your mother, that was it for me. I never looked at another woman."

"Unrequited love, eh?"

"Not exactly." He managed to look sly. "I took her to the senior ball. We went to a party at the lake after that. It was a lovely moonlit night, just perfect for walking."

"She met my father soon after that, didn't she?"

"Yes, and she never looked at me again!" He sighed sadly.

You don't know how lucky you are, I thought and smiled over at him. "You might have been my father!"

A faint blush coloured his withered cheek. "Indeed, I would have been proud to be!"

I worked my way around the room, greeting the friends of my parents' generation, and gradually the room emptied of people.

My brother closed the door behind the last visitor. "Well, that's finally over with," he said. "I wonder why they call them mourners? They sure weren't doing much mourning!"

"I expect it's their only excuse to get out of the nursing home and have something decent to eat and drink," I observed sourly. "Did you see that Mr. Brown? I'll bet he had five helpings! I don't know where he put it all!"

"D'you remember when he used to be a stout man?" My brother led the way into the dining room and began rummaging about in the various covered dishes to find what remained for our supper.

"I can still remember the first time I saw him. I was only six years old. Father bought your life insurance from him." I ran the slotted serving spoon through the pot of juice searching for a morsel of sausage.

"Ah, yes, the life insurance. It stood me in good stead."

"It paid for your education such as it was," I snorted. "I had to scrounge for mine." I thought of the years I'd worked as a secretary with just my typing and shorthand class from high school while my brother wasted the opportunities I would have just about died for. "It took me over ten years to get a Bachelor of Business and a Master's in English!"

My brother looked at me curiously. "Are you still angry about that?"

"Wouldn't you be?" I stopped sifting the juice and stared belligerently back. "I was Father's little princess from as long as I could remember until you came along! Then everything changed!" I dropped the spoon back into the pot with an angry clang. "After you came along I had to be the big girl, and do everything right, and not complain. The reason I remember the day Mr. Brown was there so well was because that was the day I discovered that girls weren't worth anything!"

"And you've been trying to prove otherwise ever since," observed my brother softly.

Tears roughened my voice and I cleared my throat angrily. "Much good it did me. I can remember asking Mother if they were going to buy life insurance for me, and she said 'Girls don't need life insurance. They only get married and keep house. They don't need an education.'" A sob slipped past my control. "It seems like all I've done all my life is try to make her proud of me." The rest of my control slid away like the pebbles sliding into the grave, and sob followed painful sob.

My brother's arms came around me. "And you did succeed. She was very proud of you. She was always bragging about you to her friends."

"Why couldn't she have told me too?" I sobbed

into his lapel. "Everything I did was to try to please her. I could have married David and had a family of my own, but oh, no, it was too important to succeed at my career, so I told him no, and for what? So I can spend a lonely old age? I feel as if I've spent my whole life looking for her and her approval and they never came."

The tears slowed to a trickle and the sobbing ceased. My brother handed me his crumpled handkerchief. I looked up at him sadly. "I'm sixty-seven years old and I'm still looking for my mother!"

Home is a Strange Country

I hope things have changed! Martha's stomach curled in excitement and apprehension as the plane rolled to a gentle stop at Pearson Airport. I've been away seven years, surely they'll be glad to see me. Well, Daddy will at least. The fasten seat belt sign flickered once and then went off. Martha sighed as she gathered her belongings.

Moments later inside the terminal, Martha threw her arms around both her parents at once. Tears weren't far from her eyes. "I sure missed you guys."

Her father cleared his throat. "It's been almost seven years. That's a long time! Let me look at you!" He held her out at arm's length. "You're so thin!" He frowned at her. "Is the heat too much for you over there?"

Martha laughed. "No, Daddy. I just eat a lot of fruit and vegetables. It's easier that way, I don't have to cook."

"A good home cooked meal is what you need," sniffed her mother. "You and Rose! The both of you! This starving yourself is no good for you!"

"Oh, Mom! Now you know you'd never say that to Rose. And anyway, I don't starve myself."

"Well, Rose's career depends on her being slender," replied her mother flushing slightly. The roar of a jet engine covered her words.

"C'mon, let's get my bag and you can tell me all about her. Is she still in New York? Is she still living with Gerry? You know she almost never writes to me." Martha grabbed their hands and headed toward the baggage carousel. "Has she been home lately?"

"No, nor likely to be either." Her father's voice was sad. "She's trying to make the switch from modelling to movies, so she's pretty busy. She used to call home at least once every few weeks or so, now she hardly calls at all."

"She's been on the cover of both *Women's Journal*, and *Women's Fashion* just since January." Her mother's face glowed with pride. "And last week they interviewed her and her photographer on that new talk show. Oh, what do they call it?" She searched her memory. "Penny's Parlour! That's what it is. She looked good."

"If you call skin and bones looking good," said her father shortly. The baggage carousel began to turn. "Which one's yours?"

In a few minutes they were driving down the expressway toward home. Martha's eyes felt stretched as she tried to take everything in at once.

"There've been quite a few changes around here!" she said. "What's that big building over there?"

"That's the new hospital," replied her father. "Your friend Sandra is the director of nursing there now."

"Well, I'll have to go and see her. She's certainly come up in the world in the last seven years."

"Seven years is more than half a decade," said her mother. "You could've been the assistant DON there now if you'd stayed around and studied like Sandra did. Her mother's so proud of her!"

"Well, I never wanted to be a nurse," said Martha trying to ignore her mother's criticism. "I expect she had to go back to school to get the necessary credentials."

"Oh, yes, she did, and did very well too, so her mother says. I guess she led her class."

"Good for her!" Martha's tone was almost too hearty. Her father threw her one of his bright blue glances with just the beginning of a wink. Martha swallowed her words of defence. "How is Mrs. Petman, anyway?" she asked instead. Her father nodded almost imperceptibly in approval.

"Oh, Angela's the same as ever. Busy all the time. She's into politics now, you know. Got her fingers into almost everything around here. Of course, that doesn't stop her from bragging up Sandra all the time." Her mother sniffed.

The car slowed as they glided up the exit ramp

onto Gilman Street. Martha sat up straighter and looked at everything excitedly. The high school where she had attended seemed smaller and dirtier than she remembered it. The oak tree they used to stand under to gossip about the boys was gone, its absence giving the schoolyard a barren look. Patches of grass poked through the asphalt where the green lawn used to be. The Marquette apartments where Sandra and her mother had lived were gone as well. In their place was a strip mall with all of the stores vacant except the laundromat and the convenience store. Martha felt a wave of depression come over her. Two more blocks and her father turned right, then shortly left, then pulled into their own driveway.

"Welcome home, Marty," he said huskily.

"Thanks, Dad," she replied, tears suddenly forming at the sound of his old nickname for her. She swallowed hard and hopped out of the car. She stood looking at the house for a few minutes noticing things about it that she had never seen before. The roof had a slight sway to the ridge that hadn't been there when she had left seven years ago. The apple tree she had grown from a seed when she was five looked straggly and worm eaten. It was never much good for apples anyway, she thought sadly, but the flowers sure smelled pretty in the spring. Her mother's flower gardens across the front of the house had been planted with evergreen shrubs. "The flowers are too much trouble anymore," her mother had written.

Her father carried her bag onto the porch and opened the front door. "Go on in, then," he urged. "Your room is just the way you left it."

Martha hurried upstairs and opened the door to her bedroom. The windows were still hung with the pink frilly curtains she'd chosen when she was twelve. They were very faded now. The same rag rug was on the floor by the bed. Her stuffed animals sat staring sightlessly into space where she had last propped them along the head of the bed. She shivered and went to look in the wrinkled mirror. "I don't look very different," she muttered. "Maybe there really is such a thing as a time warp!" She shivered again and sat observing her face in the looking glass.

It was a pleasant, happy face with clear skin tanned to a soft beige by the African sun. The cheek bones were more pronounced since last she had noticed. Maybe I am too thin, she thought turning slightly to see what she could of her profile. Well, I certainly haven't improved with age! I wonder what people see in me? I wonder why they call me pretty? The glow of inner joy that was so apparent to others was not evident to her searching eyes.

"I've brought up your suitcase." Martha started at the sound of her father's voice. "Your mother's made coffee. Will you have some?"

Martha nodded. "Let's have it in the garden. The swing is still there?"

"I had it repaired just for you. Come down when you're ready."

A few minutes later Martha joined her father on the swing. "Mom's getting supper ready," she said settling herself cross-legged on the cushion.

"She'll be out in a minute," her father replied. He set the swing into gentle motion. "So tell me about Africa," he prompted. "Is it what you expected?"

Martha smiled. "No, it's not what I expected. It's so different I hardly know where to start."

"Tell me about your school then." He sat very still waiting for her to begin.

"Well, my school is practically open air. Everything in the village is open air, otherwise it would be too hot. We get a lovely breeze morning and evening and that's when we do lessons. I have all the grades but there's not always someone in every grade so that gives me a little break. There was another teacher there for one term but she couldn't stand the bugs and snakes and the other creepy crawly things that occasionally joined us in our bunks so she went home." Martha chuckled. "The last straw was when one of the students made her a present of a tame monkey and he started grooming her. Poor Daniel was just insulted when she made him take it back. He'd raised it from infancy and it was the greatest thing he had to give her."

"It must be fairly easy to get in to the village, is it?" Her father gave another gentle push to the swing.

"Not really." Martha sipped her coffee. "It's about twenty miles into the jungle by Land Rover, and the roads aren't good. They keep trimming the trees and bushes back but it's a never-ending job."

"What's a never-ending job?" asked her mother setting her own coffee cup on the arm of the lawn chair and drying her hands on the tail of her apron.

"Keeping the jungle roads in shape," replied Martha. "One good rainstorm undoes weeks of hard work sometimes."

"I don't know how you can live in such conditions," she sniffed. "It's not at all like you were brought up."

Martha suppressed a sigh. "I have everything I need where I am," she explained patiently. "I have a roof over my head, enough food to eat, clothes on my back, and a job that I enjoy. What more could I want?"

"A home and family? I'd like to have a grandchild before I die." Her mother's voice had taken on a sour note.

"I have a home. I have a very pleasant bungalow and one of the village women keeps it for me in return for me teaching her to read. I have a glorious view over the valley from my back porch, and a front row seat for all the doings in the village on the front porch. I even have a swing."

"Who built you the swing?" asked her father.

"One of the traders. When I'd been there for awhile and he figured I was going to stay he came one day with the lumber and chains on his truck and put it up. It was after all the fuss over Lisa's departure had settled. He was the one who drove me to the village in the first place. The first thing I said when I saw where I would be living was, 'What a wonderful place for a swing!' And he remembered!" Martha smiled at the memory of her delight when he had brought the swing.

"Is he interested?" demanded her mother ever on the lookout for a man for her daughter.

"Interested?" Martha was momentarily puzzled, then she began to laugh. "No, he's not interested. He's married to a native woman. He has sixteen children who come in from the jungle to my school." She pictured George's weathered whiskery face and smiled. "He must be at least fifty. So I guess you'll have to wait for Rose to give you a grandchild."

"Rose has enough to do keeping up with that modelling career of hers, a baby would be the ruination of her figure. Besides, she and Gerry aren't even married and by the look of things I doubt they ever will be. Rose dropped us a note the other day to say she'd just signed on with that big modelling agency in New York." Her mother tried to suppress the look of pride that crossed her face. "She's got so many irons in the fire right now she wouldn't have time to get married. Half the time she isn't even in the country."

"Well, she still has a few years before she has to start listening for her alarm clock," soothed Martha. "She may come through for you yet."

"Humph, I won't hold my breath." Her mother folded her arms abruptly across her chest. "Now you could come home and find yourself a nice man and settle down and have a couple of kids before your alarm clock rings." She pursed her lips. "In fact, if you wanted to, you needn't even go back."

Martha looked at her mother in alarm. "Not go back!" The mission school and the happy faces of her pupils rose up in her mind's eye. Dom with his gap-toothed grin. He'd lost the tooth when he'd gotten struck in the mouth while they were learning to play baseball. She'd had to pull the root herself with instructions over the radio from the dentist in the city. Another tooth would grow there eventually, but it would be a year or two and it might never be straight.

Marthy's face with its sparkling eyes was special. She'd helped deliver her when the doctor couldn't get there and her mother had been too weak to deliver her without help. Her mother had named her for Miss Martha, as the children all called her. Marthy had just started school this year. She'd insisted on going with her big brother to be near Miss Martha. All the others were special too for one reason or another. She couldn't not go back. She wasn't just the teacher to these people, she was nurse and doctor and dentist too. And they were more than her friends. Why, the whole village had turned out to see her off in George's old truck. The children had set up an awful wail when they saw that she was really leaving. It had taken her almost ten minutes to reassure them that she wasn't leaving forever.

"Martha, this is your home," her mother was saying as Martha slowly recovered from the wrench that the idea of never returning had given her. "This is your home and that's only where you work. Now if you were beautiful or had a real job like your sister and could earn a decent living it'd be a different thing, but you can't, and don't try to tell me you can either. You'll die a poor and lonely old maid in a foreign country if you keep on like this."

Martha said nothing. What's there to say to a remark like that? she asked herself sadly. Rose has always been the beautiful one and the apple of Mom's eye. I was never able to live up to her even though I'm the oldest. Well, at least I know for sure now where I stand.

Her mother stood up and smoothed her apron over her plump belly. "I'll just go and set the table. Dinner'll be ready in about ten minutes." She headed back across the lawn.

Presently the kitchen light came on and Martha could see her moving about doing supper chores. A wave of almost hatred nearly overwhelmed Martha. The sensation was so strong it made her faintly sick.

Her father cleared his throat awkwardly. "Don't you mind your mother, Martha. She suffers from a lack of tact sometimes. She really does want the best for you."

Martha compressed her lips. "I won't Dad." How long it will take before I really don't mind, she wondered.

SECOND SIGHT

Reading the Cards

Fortune telling is a strange business. I used to read regular deck playing cards. Those whom I read for said I was accurate, but who knows why or how. After much thought it seems to me that fortune telling has nothing to do with the cards or the tea leaves, or anything else you choose to use. I think it has to do with your ability to concentrate and tune into other people, not the tools you use to help you to focus your attention. I have often "read" people without cards and quite accidentally. I remember the look of shock on one woman's face when I mentioned something that was pertinent to her private story. I had never met her before and out popped a remark about her life and conditions. Shocked me too!

Another woman I was minimally acquainted with began to avoid me. I was getting too close to the truth of her life. She had a look of fear in her eyes when she'd see me coming and if she could, she would go the other way.

I went to a Tarot reader once. A nurse colleague of mine was eager to go and have her cards read. It was actually on Friday, May the 13th. No one would go with her but me. So off we went. She was read first. Then I decided to do it too.

The reading was very much on the mark. The reader told me all about a man I would meet soon. The words she used were, "become aware of a man in September." This was more accurate than "meet," as I had already made his acquaintance and for interpersonal reasons I didn't much like him.

At this point I thought to myself, I'll just see how good she is, so I asked her what he looked like. Height, hair colour, eye colour, she was absolutely accurate. She said he was sometimes in the country and sometimes not. True again. She couldn't decide whether he was a doctor or not. He would be supportive of my work, at that time nursing. In fact, he's not a medical doctor, he's a Ph.D. and he is very supportive of my writing as he was when I was nursing. There were many other points. They were all true, but the real clincher came when on the last Sunday in August he came and sat with me in church. He had just returned from his bicycle trip to France and I came to discover that he had spent several years studying in France, and on his time off he'd travelled around Europe. We were married in April of the following year. We have now been happily married for thirty-five years.

Out of the Corner of my Eye

I am unusually sensitive, so it would seem. I can hear things that haven't been said, I sometimes see things that aren't there. I can read the mood of a room. Sometimes I hear whole orchestras, classical music I've never heard in real life, Jazz, blues and fiddles. I was baby-sitting my nephew one night and heard music all evening long. In this case it was jazz. I asked my sister when they got home if she had left a radio on. I couldn't find it to change the channel or turn it off. All she said was: "Don't start that stuff around here." So I never did find out the source of the evening's entertainment. The whole business was entirely random.

Once as I was waking, I heard the piano in the next room play a series of five distinct notes as clear and beautiful as if someone had actually played them. In fact, they were so real that I thought my husband had played them. Oops! Neither had he played them, nor had he heard them. I hurried out to capture them while I could still remember them. I have never heard that particular sequence of notes before nor since. I'm sure it's embedded in the ether somewhere.

I once lived in a basement apartment at a friend's house for a few months. She was involved with a metaphysical religion that believed in ascended masters. She introduced me to it and I read up on its teachings and shortly thereafter I "met" one of the masters. Actually it was two of them standing side by side in the corner of the room smiling benignly at me. They were wearing burnt orange robes and scared the wits out of me. It was about then that I decided to find another place to live.

When I close my eyes what I see are bright white balls of light. Some big, some not so big. They float and dance as if their lives depended on it. They don't seem to know that all I have to do is blink and they disappear and new ones take their places. Someone once told me that they were my guides. What guides? I don't have guides! Never heard of such things!

Of course, I hadn't heard of them. My family doesn't talk of such things even though a goodly number of us can claim having at least a passing acquaintance with "the second sight." That's what the old people called it. Officially it's called pre-cognition. I don't usually admit it any more than the old people did. People tend to look at you strangely if you even hint at such a thing. Those are the ones who aren't sensitive like that, mainly because they don't pay attention in a gently held sort of way that's difficult to explain. It's more than just knowing who's calling before you pick up the telephone receiver. For me, it's more like snapshots in my mind.

Before I Was Born

I have always been here in some form or other. I remember as a toddler lying in my crib at night and listening to the planes flying over on their way to Shearwater Naval Air Base in Dartmouth and being very afraid. I somehow knew that planes dropped bombs. I also knew what bombs did.

I was born two years after the end of World War Two, so my knowing about this with such accuracy is a little eerie in one so young. I realized later that the adults were still quite preoccupied with the war. It was probably the biggest excitement they had ever known in their lives, so perhaps I absorbed it from ambient conversations as children do. I had the same reaction when the blimps came over Halifax a few years later. It raised an uneasy worry in my childish mind: Is there going to be another war?

Many years later I met a man. When he walked into the room it was as if a snapshot came down and was superimposed on the present day scene. The picture was of him and me and two little children, a boy and a girl. I was begging him not to go. He was insisting he had to. It was at the very beginning of a war. I had the sense of being in

London. I was dressed in 30's attire as were the children. I was slender with black wavy hair tied back in a bun. I had seen a psychic a few years prior to this event and she had told me that I had died at a young age of a broken heart. The year she named was 1945. Reincarnation? Whatever it was, it was definitely eerie.

Cats I Have Known

There have been many cats in my life, all of them dear companions. They each had their own quirks of personality that made them memorable. I usually adopt my kitties in pairs.

Gabby was a sleek, charcoal grey cat whom I acquired at the PEI Humane Society over thirty years ago. He had a sister Babe, who came along with him. Gabby was a confident, swaggering male, quite sure of his lovability and his place in the universe. When we moved west I made other arrangements for him with an older couple who doted on him, even providing him with a summer camp by the lake where he could hunt in the woods or bask in the sun as he chose.

We went back to visit a couple of times over the years. Each time he was delighted to see me. On the first occasion, after an absence of four years, he was napping upstairs when we came. I called him as I always had and I heard his feet hit the floor immediately and the kitty footsteps came pounding down the stairs. He came and stretched up to me and I picked him up and he put his "arms" around my neck as had been his habit. Later in the evening he came and stretched his full length along my thigh as close as he could get and just stayed there as if communing with me. It was almost spiritual the connection we had. When we were leaving, he was walking up the hill toward the road he turned his head and looked back at me with a sad resigned expression as if to say: "You're leaving me again."

He eventually developed colon cancer and had to be put to sleep. Mary said that she held his paw while the deed was done, then scattered his ashes at the camp under the bird feeder where he'd spent so many hours.

Kitty was another confident male who adopted us when we first went to Missouri. He was obviously someone's pet who'd been abandoned or strayed, as he had been neutered. He came to my husband on the front porch with burdocks in his belly fur. He lay on his back and purred and allowed John to pick them out one by one. He seemed to want to be with us and moved right in. He came with us when we moved to our own house. He, who had always lived on the streets, became exclusively a house kitty. He was a dear fellow too, but as it happened he developed a mouth sore that only responded to female hormone. One of the possible side effects was the potential to become diabetic and, of course, he did. We did the best we could but Kitty didn't survive.

Then came Taffy and Sandy. These were also

Humane Society kitties. Sandy was a little feral all her life and never really became a comfortable house cat. Taffy, on the other hand, was a cuddler. After she became an only cat she developed a little bedtime routine where she would lie by my right shoulder after I got in bed. When I had finished my bedtime reading she would "kiss" me good-night with a tiny lick just under my lower lip and go to the bottom of the bed. In her elder years she became very ill with no hope of recovery so she too went to sleep.

Taffy's passing was very sad and I was determined never to have another cat. Then two weeks after her demise, 9/11 occurred. I couldn't get through that without a kitty to talk to. A day or so later I had the strongest urge to go to the Humane Society. It was so strong that I could not ignore it. So off we went and found the remaining two kittens of a surrendered litter. One was fat and fluffy, and the other was sleek and slender. Both were white with black tails. One could purr, the other could only squeak. One was also a talker. Such conversations as we would have, but she always had to have the last word.

We took them home and I named the sleek one who talked and purred, Molly, and the chubby squeaker, Lucy, after the main characters in my first novel, *Shades of Molly*. They travelled with us when we moved to PEI from Missouri. Molly was never a completely well kitty. Not sick, but just not well. She developed a cancerous tumour in her chest and had to be put to sleep just before Christmas one year. Lucy lives on and is still chubby. She finally learned to do more than squeak and can hold quite an articulate conversation. She has adjusted very well to being an only cat and has also developed a substantial purr.

Cats are very knowing animals especially if you have a relationship with them. They seem to be telepathic. I felt very sad about putting my kitties to sleep but I "saw" Kitty after his demise. He was standing on top of the hill on Lightburne Street all lit up by the morning sun. His red and blond fur was shining as if back lit and he looked so healthy and happy. He was turned sideways to me and was looking straight at me. Then he gave a little hop and ran off down the other side of the hill with his tail in the air. It was almost as if to say: " See, I'm okay, Mom." I was comforted.

Molly also came to me several days after her passing too. She actually spoke to me. She said: "Thanks, Mom, I feel so much better now." There was a whole semi-circle of cats in silhouette behind her. I think I recognized Gabby. I had the sense that I knew the others too.

House Fire

Mid-evening, July 3rd, 1975: I was having my second cup of coffee with Genevieve, my neighbour across the road when people driving by saw the smoke coming out of the eaves, and the flames through the window. My house was burning!

It was an eerie thing. The whole time we were building the house I kept having a nagging intuition that it would burn. I dismissed the idea as just fearful fancies. What could I do about it anyway?

A few days before the fire I was out weeding the garden. Genevieve came across the road and invited me to coffee. She drank a lot of coffee—me not so much, but I went. Weeding gets monotonous. When I left her house after our cup together, I forgot to take my gloves with me. Several times that week I thought of them. It got to where after the third or fourth self-reminder and forgetting, it came to me that there must be a reason why I left them there. It seems it was a ploy by my guardians to get me out of the house and keep me safely away.

The eeriness does not end there. The evening before the fire I was visiting neighbours about a mile away but I could see my house across the fields. There was a pressure all around me and I kept looking across at my house saying: "My house is going to burn! My house is going to burn!" The friends kept telling me I was imagining things but by this time I was actually seeing it burn. It was as if a snapshot descended in front of my eyes of me standing down in the front yard with the house burning inside, mainly in the living room. There were a lot of people standing around watching it but no fire trucks.

As I thought about it over the years I have come to realize how accurate my intuitions and mystical snapshots were. The house only burned in the living room where the fire started, the rest of the house was very smoke damaged and required stripping. There were no fire trucks there because they got lost! They did get there eventually and put what was left of the fire out. It had almost smothered itself by that time. That was forty years ago, and the garden never did get weeded.

Northern Lights and Eclipses of the Moon

We don't often see the northern lights except in pictures. Last night they filled the northern sky with a gentle wash of colours. The only time I have ever seen them was about thirty-five years ago in the middle of winter. They were undulating ribbons of transparent white suspended vertically in the dark sky over the Island. It seemed as if they were just out of reach. But who would want to touch them and spoil their delicate luminosity? Certainly not I, but I know some would be up there playing in them if they could. It would be like being the first to drive across a pristine field of new snow on a winter's day.

There are many strange things happening in the sky lately. Individually they are not strange, but taken together there is room for the imagination to take over and build all kinds of stories around them. A few weeks ago we had a lunar eclipse that occurred early enough to actually watch. It was the night of the supermoon, a time when the moon is in closest orbit to the earth. It took awhile to completely manifest but at its height, the moon turned orange. It was as if a great round of cheese was suspended in the sky over the West River. It disproved the ancient nursery lore that the moon is made of green cheese. Thank goodness, I much prefer cheddar.

As for strange events occurring, has anyone besides me seen lights in the sky? Little flashes now and again in the darkness? They are so quick that my eyes barely catch them before they are gone. Someone told me once that they are guardian angels or guides. I must have a lot of them for that to be true. They might only be a trick of my eyesight. Who knows? I have seen long steady lights that parade in majesty, high among the stars. Someone told me those were satellites. Maybe. They are too far away to tell. What if they're not? Who is this know-it-all someone who informs us with such authority and spoils my fun?

After Dark

I don't like the darkness. It's not the darkness so much as being in it, especially by myself. I have been in darkness so complete that I couldn't even see the path I was walking on. There was no moon, no stars were visible, not that stars cast much light anyway. It was in the country so there were no street lights. The people I was with were of no help. They were country people who were familiar with profound darkness and wouldn't even offer me an arm. I stumbled along following the sound of their voices until we found the road. It was at the edge of a wood, so was even more deeply in darkness.

I don't really know where this unease with darkness began. I can't think of any triggering event even in childhood. I just know that I lived in a house once that seemed haunted. I would do all my bedtime chores, go in to my bedroom, close the door, and sleep with the light on. If I had to "go" after that, I did so with great trepidation and procrastination. I would open the bedroom door quietly and "they" would be in the hallway laughing at me and scorning me. These disembodied faces were unrecognizable as anyone I knew.

I'd reach carefully around the door frame and flip the hall switch and they would vanish. This was totally irrational as the bathroom door was almost directly across the hall. Two steps would have taken me there.

The house was a normal sunny house during the day but at night it became sinister. There seemed to be one entity in particular overseeing the antics and one day I decided that I'd had enough. I was taking a bus ride to Halifax which was about two hundred miles away. I mentally said to it, "You're coming with me." And I had the sense that it did. For the first part of the ride no one shared the seat with me. We arrived in Middleton at the bus stop and I again said to it: "This is as far as you go." It got up and left, and I was never bothered by it again. The other faces never manifested again either, and for the rest of the trip I had a seat mate all the way.

My experiences have led me to write some short stories about second sight and premonitions. Two of them follow.

Second Sight

Spring on the Square had been another rousing success. Both Cindy and I had done well despite the noise and confusion of the crowds that walked past our tents eating funnel cakes. They licked their sticky fingers and peered into the relative darkness of the kiosks set up around the perimeter of the square. The odour of barbecue and popcorn pervaded the air and despite breakfast I had longed for lunch and later on supper. Across the street, on the courthouse lawn, children played Frisbee and catch to the mortal danger of the passersby. The day was nearly over, and the crowds were thinning as the sun turned the horizon a brilliant orange that reflected in the coffee house windows turning them to day-glo colours too. I gathered my Tarot cards and folded up my table before popping in on Cindy in the next tent.

Cindy bent her curly blond head over her crystal ball. She looked more like the heroine of a grocery store romance novel than a seer of well-earned repute. "I see you owning a very large house by the end of the year," she said, quite matter-of-factly. "In fact, probably by the end of September."

"Oh, go on!" I scoffed. "How would I ever get a house? Half the time I have trouble making the rent!"

"Well," she replied a trifle huffily, "that's what I see." She began to pull the black velvet cover over the polished crystal.

"Cindy," I wailed, "don't be like that. Tell me more."

She hesitated a moment.

"C'mon Cindy," I begged. "Please. At least tell me where the money's coming from to buy it."

She shrugged one shoulder, uncovered the crystal again and began her detached stare into its clear depths. Our talents were similar, but I couldn't see things for myself, and especially not in the gazing ball. Cindy seemed to have just the knack for that, but she couldn't read cards. My insights came to me in the form of waking dreams and premonitions. I also read Tarot cards. Cindy earned her living at scrying. I would have starved.

Cindy's face took on the vacant look it sometimes did when she was almost in trance. "I see a short, dark man standing beside a gate. He's waving. There's a woman on the other side of the gate. She seems to be waiting for him." Cindy began to rock back and forth still staring into the crystal. "There's an aura of incompleteness about the man. I get the sense of a wasted life somehow, and now he's leaving." Her breathing became laboured. "I have such a feeling of breathlessness." She was almost gasping. "He's filled with regrets, but he doesn't see how he could have made it any different. It's as if he's been stuck emotionally all these years." She breathed a deep sigh. "He's turning to the woman and they're walking away. He's looking back again and waving."

"Is he someone I know?" My own breath wasn't very stable either. Cindy and I had a reading day for each other twice a year right after the two festivals that were held on the square, spring and fall. It hadn't been this intense since just before my mother died.

She sighed deeply and sat back in her folding chair. "I don't know," she replied. "I didn't get a sense of him knowing you well, but I also didn't get a sense of him being a stranger." She drew another deep breath and ran her fingers through her short yellow curls. "Phew! I'm glad I only get that kind of connection now and again. My heart's just pounding!"

I pondered the possibilities of the reading for several weeks but nothing came of them and the whole business gradually slipped into the background of my life. For once Cindy was wrong, I thought, as I arranged photographs for my album one evening. It was a job I hated, but I loved to take pictures so there was always a stack of them sitting around on side tables and in cupboards, waiting to be sorted and put away. Some of them were so old I had to consult my journal to give them a date and location.

"There!" I patted the last one into its place and began to leaf backwards through the album. "Goodness, I didn't realize these pictures were in here," I muttered. I examined them more closely. Why, that's Peter and his sister, Edith! A sense of sadness crept over me and Edith's face wavered and lost its definition. It's been ten years since she died. It only seems like last week. I blinked and the photo came back into focus. I turned the page, and pictures of the two years I had spent in Little Brook brought the memories rushing back.

It was fun while it lasted, I thought, then remembered the colossal fight Peter and I had had just before I left for Charlottetown. "I never could depend on you," I grumbled at his picture. "All you ever wanted to do was read and smoke that damned pipe of yours, and imagine yourself an intellectual." The old anger oozed its way back into my consciousness. Some of it had been left over from the disaster of my one and only marriage, and Peter had been the recipient of that, besides earning a goodly portion of his own. I stared hard at the photo. "Well, I guess you were a friend when I most needed you," I said reluctantly. The picture seemed to smile in agreement. "And we did have some good discussions. I miss those, and I miss visiting with Edith."

As I continued holding the photo in relaxed attention it appeared to darken and Peter no longer seemed to smile. A sense of deep depression overcame me. Like a photograph in my mind's eye, I could see the blackness of storm clouds gathering and boiling about the head of my former friend. The sense of doom and disaster were almost overwhelming. It was the way the second sight operated in me. I slammed the book shut and the mood lightened somewhat, but I was restless and unhappy for the rest of the evening.

The mood stayed with me for several weeks. The mental picture of Peter with his head embroiled in the thunderstorm kept interposing itself between me and my work. It came to occupy my attention both waking and sleeping, until I was so exhausted and crabby that my boss called me aside and had a "chat" with me about office relationships. "If you don't do something about your condition, I will," she said in steel-gentle tones.

"You will, too," I muttered to myself in the mirror that evening. My unhappy blue eyes looked back at me from their surrounding circles of black. "Oof, I look awful! It's no wonder she's after me!" As I stared at my reflection, the familiar image of Peter and his storm clouds superimposed itself on my face. "All right! All right!! I'll call you!" The image faded, and I stomped to the telephone.

Peter answered on the first ring. "Katie! It's so good to hear your voice!" His own collapsed into a spasm of loose coughing.

"Yours too," I muttered. "How are you?"

"Fine, fine." His gurgling breath rattled down the wire. "Are you in Little Brook?"

"No, I'm in Charlottetown," I replied, wanting to clear my throat for him. "Are you sure you're all right?"

"As well as a dying man can be."

"C'mon, Peter, cut it out!" I was still resentful at having been forced into calling him when I had resolved not to speak to him again in this lifetime.

"No, it's true. I have lung cancer. The doctors in Halifax gave me six months to live. If I took chemo, they said I might see Christmas. It's disseminating, so there's not much chance no matter what I do." He coughed again. "It's sure good to hear from you. What made you decide to call?"

"Second sight!" I snapped, angry again at this turn of events. "I suppose you're still smoking."

"Of course! What difference will it make now?"

I sighed. "None, I suppose. Are you by yourself?"

"Just me and the dog and the great-grandchildren of Edith's six cats."

His chuckle ended in another paroxysm of coughing. I tried to breathe for him. "Do you need someone to stay with you?" My voice was tinged with anger and efficiency.

"Not in that tone of voice I don't," he replied, "but thanks for asking. Dying is something you do on your own no matter how many people are standing around." He was silent for a moment and I could hear him breathing. "Would you come and stay with me?" he asked.

He was fishing. I knew the tone of voice well. "No, I can't. I'd have to leave my job, and it's a good one." I felt mean, as if I was refusing the dying man's last request. In a sense I was, but I knew the kind of heartache close involvement with him could bring, and I wasn't up for that. He was passive aggressive, and I'd suffered under his less than tender manipulations in the past.

"Well, I guess there's no more to be said." He coughed again, wetly. "So this is likely goodbye."

"It seems so." Now that the moment was actually here I was reluctant to let him go. He heard the reluctance.

"Are you certain you won't come and stay with me? It would sure make the journey easier."

"No! No, I can't." It took all my strength to deny

him. I swallowed hard. "Say hello to Edith when you see her."

"Will do," he replied. "Thanks for calling."

The image of Peter and his storm clouds ceased to bother me after the phone call, and I was able to put him and his predicament into the back closets of my mind. At least for awhile. The dreams started again in August and by mid-September I'd had another warning from the boss. The fierce glint in her eye told me she meant business this time. There's not much I can do about it, I thought morosely as I climbed into bed for another restless night. I lay there and stared at the ceiling for what seemed like hours. In fact, as the room lightened, I thought it was dawn.

"Ooh," I groaned, and rolled onto my other side. "I can't stand this much longer."

"Can't stand what?" It was Peter's voice!

"So now you're talking to me too," I grumbled.

"Turn over and look at me," he demanded. "I haven't much time."

I turned onto my back and cautiously opened my eyes. Peter's face with its cloud of black hair seemed to be floating between me and the ceiling. His slight body was just a suggestion behind it.

"It's okay, I'm really here. I just wanted you to know that I passed over tonight. Edith met me. She says hello. I'm fine now. It's nice to be able to breathe again. Take care." His form began to dissipate.

"Wait, Peter, wait!" It was too late. He disappeared into the ceiling. "Well! Isn't that just like him! Elusive as ever!" I turned onto my side again and plumped my pillow. Then I fell into the best sleep I'd had in weeks.

After a few days life was nearly back to normal. The dark circles disappeared, and people began to be less edgy when I was around. Even the boss smiled at me approvingly one day.

"Pretty official looking letter," she commented, dropping the long white envelope onto my desk. "Maybe someone died and left you his fortune."

"I doubt that," I replied, "I don't know anyone rich enough to leave anyone anything, least of all me. They probably just want me for jury duty!" I tore open the envelope.

"Holy smoke! You're right! Peter left me the farm!"

Night Duty

Enoch Price lay on his back in the recliner by the nurses' station waving his scrawny arms in the air and apparently talking to himself.

"Enoch! Be quiet. It's midnight and time you were asleep." Nurse Susan got up from her charts and went to Enoch's side. "D'you need anything, Enoch?" She tucked the blanket closer to his whiskery chin.

Enoch looked at her for a moment then reached out a crabbed hand and tweaked her cheek. "A pretty lady and some malt whiskey like my granddaddy used to make back in the glen." He grinned a toothless grin and then blew her a kiss. "I'll remember you to God. I'll be seeing him soon, you know." He sighed and began again to wave his hands in the air. "Of course, I may go to the hot place." His expression became glum.

"Oh, Enoch, why would a nice man like you be sent there?"

"I wasn't always a nice man," said Enoch. "I did a very evil thing in my youth. It created a lot of unhappiness and now I have to pay for it." His eyes wandered away from her face and his expression became vague. He began to sing a hymn with a somewhat recognizable tune.

Susan smoothed his sparse grey hair and tucked the blankets more closely around his skinny body. "It sounds as if you've already paid for it, Enoch," she whispered and returned to her charting.

Enoch lay mumbling to himself and waving his arms. The ward was dark and quiet with the first deep sleep of the night. I wish they'd come for me, he thought, my arms are getting tired. He thought of how wonderful it would be to be with Mary again then swallowed hard against the tears of loneliness as he remembered their life together. Maybe I shouldn't be so eager to go, he thought, and a spasm of guilt and fear clutched at his insides.

The lights by the elevator brightened as the door opened and a figure stepped out.

"Hello, Enoch!" said the man in doctor's whites. "You can stop waving your arms now, it's almost time to go."

Enoch stopped waving. His arms remained suspended in mid-air as he stared at the doctor. "I know you!" he said. "You're the doctor who sat with me all night that time I had the fever when I was a boy." He peered at the man's name tag. "Dr. Gabriel."

"That's right, Enoch. I'm flattered that you remember me."

"Well, you haven't changed a bit. You're as young as ever."

Dr. Gabriel smiled. "Where I live people don't age rapidly."

"'S'at so?" Enoch pondered this idea in silence for some moments. "It must be the water. Not too many of them free radicals floating around in it."

"Something like that." Dr. Gabriel laughed and settled himself on the sofa beside Enoch's recliner. "Have you enjoyed your stay here?"

Enoch shrugged as well as he could in his position. "The nurses are good. At least most of them. The food's not bad. Three squares a day. They needn't send me any more of that cold jiggly red stuff. Jello they call it. Give me some good bread pudding like Mary used to make." He sighed. "I threw that jello stuff at the dietician one day. Only missed her by an inch!" He giggled at the memory then sighed again. "Mary wouldn't have approved. 'Course I didn't think of that at the time." His face drooped into lines of old grief. "I sure do miss Mary."

Dr. Gabriel smiled. "She misses you too. D'you know she's waiting for you?"

Enoch looked at his company. "My Mary? How would you know her?"

"I'm well acquainted with Mary," said Dr. Gabriel. "We've had many long chats about you."

"Well, now!" Enoch peered at his visitor. "What

did she have to say about me?" he asked.

"You needn't worry, it was all good," said Dr. Gabriel.

"Well, that's just like my Mary, never a bad word to say about anyone."

Dr. Gabriel regarded Enoch. "Would she have had anything bad to say about you?"

Enoch snorted. "She could say plenty." He shut his lips.

"Care to tell me about it?"

Enoch stared at Dr. Gabriel. His eyes were the softest, kindest eyes he had ever seen. He felt himself relax in his recliner.

"You can tell me about everything," said Dr. Gabriel.

"Not about this," said Enoch. A tear trickled down his wrinkled cheek. "I was an evil man and I made Mary suffer that day. And she suffered for a long time afterwards too."

"Enoch, you were never an evil man. Misguided perhaps, and certainly thoughtless, but not truly evil."

Enoch was little comforted. "I hurt Mary that day. Another hour and she might have died."

"But she didn't, did she."

Enoch sighed. "No thanks to me."

"You know, if you told me about it, you'd probably feel better."

"I've never told a soul about it, not even Mary.

How can I tell you?" he asked. "If Mary knew what I'd done that day she'd never forgive me."

"The truth is, Enoch, you haven't forgiven yourself, have you?"

"How could I? My sin was great that day and Mary almost died because of it."

"It wasn't all your fault, you know."

"What do you know about it?" Enoch stared at Dr. Gabriel.

"Not the details," said Dr. Gabriel. "If you told me about it maybe I could help you sort it out and it wouldn't seem so bad."

"You mean gloss it over." Enoch sniffed.

"No, I do not! I mean understand it and accept your part of the blame and forgive yourself and Mary, and let the rest go."

Enoch thought this over for a few moments then swallowed hard. "Mary and I had a disagreement just after we were married. It was a fight really. I never knew she had so much passion in her. We were so angry with one another. I stormed out and left her, intending to go to the field I was clearing and work some of it off, but I needed a piece for the harness and I stopped at the hardware store in town. I met Harriet on the way home and stopped to chat with her and one thing led to another and I never got to the field at all. Anyway, when I got home I found Mary lying beside the step ladder in the kitchen. I thought for sure she was dead. There was an awful lot of blood. She'd been pregnant with our first child and she lost it that day. It took her a long time to recover and we never had any more. She wanted children so badly." Enoch stopped talking and sighed.

"Enoch, losing the baby was an accident. It's unfortunate that it happened just that way, but you and Mary weren't meant to have any children, and you and she never fought like that again, did you?"

"No." Enoch sighed again.

Dr. Gabriel looked at Enoch. "Is there anything more you want to tell me?"

"No. Yes. That's not the whole story."

"Oh?"

"Yes. Oh, this is the worst part of it. Just a few weeks after Mary should have been giving birth, Harriet had my son. I never told Mary and I've never been able to acknowledge him, though with his bright red hair and freckles whose else could he be?"

"Mary knows about Harriet and her son. As you say, the red hair was the give-away. She went to Harriet soon after the baby was born and had a long talk with her. She offered to adopt the child but Harriet wouldn't hear of it."

Enoch gaped at Dr. Gabriel. "You mean she knew all these years?"

Dr. Gabriel nodded. "She knew and she forgave

you, and since there had already been enough heartache from your disagreement, she never let on that she knew."

"She forgave me?"

"Yes. She knew you well enough to know that it was just a momentary indiscretion and that it wouldn't likely happen again."

Enoch began to smile. "Now isn't that just like my Mary. I am a better man because of her goodness. She forgave me! When can I see her?"

"In a little while," said Dr. Gabriel. "Just a few more hours, really."

"Why not now?" Enoch demanded.

"Because it's not time yet. Tell me about this place. Have you been happy here?"

"Happy enough, I guess." Enoch watched Susan stride down the ward to answer a light. "There goes the best nurse in the whole place!"

"What makes her the best?" Dr. Gabriel cocked his head to one side and appeared to be memorizing the information on Nurse Susan.

Enoch glanced at him sharply. "Why, she just knows how to fix a fellow up. She knows how to get the pillows just right and what to say and how to say it." He thought about Susan for a moment. "She makes a fellow feel safe."

Dr. Gabriel smiled. "Do the other patients feel the same way?"

"That bunch of loonies," snorted Enoch. "They

don't even know their own names, most of them! Take that one there for instance." He pointed at Mrs. Teton wandering down the hall stark naked. "All she ever does is sleep all day and roam all night."

Susan came out of Mr. Butts' room and caught sight of Mrs. Teton just as she rounded the nurses' station. "Mrs. Teton!" Susan hurried after her. "Whatever are you doing?"

Mrs. Teton turned and looked at Susan. "Sunshine and fresh air will make them grow!" She stroked her pendulous bosom.

"Yes, and night air'll make them shrivel," said Susan. "C'mon now, and put your nightie on. You can't be walking around like this." She steered Mrs. Teton past Enoch and Dr. Gabriel.

"D'you see what I mean?" said Enoch. "Her daughter insisted on taking her home after the nurses got her all settled on medication and calmed down. She thought she could handle her. Mrs. Teton was fine for the first few days until the priest came to visit one afternoon. The daughter had forgotten to give her the noon pills and the fog was lifting. Mrs. Teton visited nicely as you please with the priest for about an hour, and when he got up to go he remarked on how pleased he was to see her so well. 'Hot dog!' she shouted and mooned him! She was back here the next day and hasn't left since." Enoch giggled, then sobered. "I knew her when she was young and she'd never have done such a thing. She was always a fine lady."

"How d'you know all this?" Dr. Gabriel chuckled.

Enoch looked sly. "They put me out here in the recliner a lot of the time and I hear lots of things I'm not supposed to hear. They think I'm senile, but I'm not. I could tell you all kinds of things." He giggled again, then frowned.

"What is it?" asked the doctor.

"Oh, just a little something I know about Nurse Susan." He pursed his lips and thought hard for a moment. "I don't suppose you could intervene?"

"Probably not," said Dr. Gabriel, "but let's hear it anyway."

"Well, I heard her telling Sandra the other night how she thought her daughter was seeing the wrong man. She has good reason for thinking it too. She was really distressed and it's a terrible shame. The daughter's a nice girl, but she doesn't have a lot of sense. She's young, you know. If I thought it would do any good, I'd speak to the daughter myself. But you know how it is, once you're labelled senile they don't believe a word that comes out of your mouth anymore." He looked sad. "Of course, in my case they may be right. I don't talk a lot of sense now. Here I am talking to you and since they can't see you, they think I'm talking to myself." He stared hard at

Dr. Gabriel. "They can't see you, can they?"

Dr. Gabriel smiled. "No, Enoch, they can't see me. I'm just here to keep you company before your departure."

"Well, that's real thoughtful of you." Enoch began plucking at the sheets and his voice fell to a murmur. "And you say I'll be seeing my Mary soon? And she really forgave me?"

"Yes, Enoch, she really forgave you, and you'll be seeing her in about an hour. She's making herself pretty for you just like she always did."

"Och," said Enoch, "she doesn't have to do that, she's always beautiful to me."

"Nevertheless," said Dr. Gabriel, "that's what she wants to do. We'll just rest here a little while longer and then it'll be time to go. It's not far, you know. Just down the hall past the elevators and through those curtains."

"What curtains?" asked Enoch. "There were never any curtains there before. That's the way to the other ward." He raised his head from his pillow and looked down the hall. "Well, now, there are curtains there! I certainly don't remember those." He peered at Dr. Gabriel. "Did you put them there?"

His companion nodded. "They're only temporary, a veil so to speak."

"Oh," said Enoch. "I see." He dropped his head back onto his pillow.

Dr. Gabriel rose to his feet. "So, are you ready? It's time to go now."

"D'you expect me to walk?" asked Enoch in surprise. "You know I haven't walked by myself in at least a year and not at all for the last three months."

"You can do it." Gabriel walked toward the light. "C'mon now, Mary's waiting."

Enoch rose from the chair. He marvelled at how light his body felt. At the door to the hallway he turned and said, "Good-by, Susan. Gabriel said he'd see about your problem. If he doesn't, I will." He turned toward the light. "And she really forgave me!"

Learn more about Margaret Westlie, her life
and her books, at
www.margaretwestlie.com
or scan the QR code below.

www.ingramcontent.com/pod-product-compliance
Lightning Source LLC
Chambersburg PA
CBHW072153090426
42740CB00012B/2252